Cover Art

Painting: *Window of Life*
Artist: Tanya Momi
Collection: Private collection of Ms. Wendy

This painting draws inspiration from the window of the room where the artist, Tanya Momi, was born — a portal between memory and the world beyond, symbolizing life's passage from past to present.

DAUGHTER OF A REFUGEE

India's Partition: History, Memory, and Art

TANYA MOMI

Executive Editor: Jaypreet Singh

INDIA • UK • USA

Connect with the Artist:
Website: TanyaMomi.com
Facebook: @tanya.momi
Instagram: @TanyaMomi
Twitter: @TanyaMomi
LinkedIn: Tanya-Momi
Email: tanya@tanyamomi.com

For more information:
Daughterofarefugee.org

Back Page Photo by Bao @baoartistry (hair & makeup by Bao)
Painting Photography by Mark Taylor @zettapix

ISBN 979-8-89171-247-8
ISBN 979-8-89171-248-5 (ebook)

TABLE OF CONTENTS

DEDICATION

To my parents, Mom & Dad: thank you for telling your stories
of hardship and loss. It planted a seed in me that is now fully
grown & ready to share with the world.

And for all the refugees around the globe.

August 15, 2027 marks the 80th anniversary of Partition. As this book remembers that date early, it contains tools and messages to support the growth for a healthy nation and a plan to build a peaceful relationship with our neighboring country, a plan that now demands the full attention and courageous action of our leaders.

Foreword
By Balbir Singh Momi

My Dearest *Beti* (daughter) Tanya:

As I sit down to write you this letter, my heart is heavy with emotions, for today marks the 75th anniversary of India's Independence, a momentous occasion that forever changed the course of our lives. I wanted to share a piece of history, a chapter from my own life, so you may better understand the significance of this day.

In the sweltering August heat of 1947, I was just a twelve-and-one-half-year-old boy and a student in the eighth grade at Khalsa High School in our village, Nawan Pind, Chak no. 78, Distt. Sheikhupura, which is now a part of Pakistan. The schools were closed for the summer break, but the air was full of the news of India's Independence and the painful division of our beloved homeland.

You see, my dear, the demand for a separate country called Pakistan was echoing loudly, led by Muslim leaders who believed in a distinct nation. The division of India was based on the ratio of the Muslim and Hindu populations, and it was a time of immense uncertainty and turmoil.

We had great leaders at the helm of our nation, guiding us through this tumultuous period. Mahatma Gandhi, Jawahar Lal Nehru, Muhammad Ali Jinnah, Sardar Patel, Baldev Singh, and Master Tara Singh were the stalwarts who navigated us through this transition. They negotiated with the British Empire for our independence, which was ultimately realized on the night of August 14, 1947.

While India celebrated its newfound freedom, it came at a tremendous cost. Millions of lives were lost, and the very essence of humanity was tested. The population exchange that followed the Partition led to Hindus and Sikhs being forced out of Pakistan, leaving their homes and possessions behind. Similarly, many Muslims left India to make Pakistan their new home. This mass migration left an indelible mark on our history.

The Sikh and Hindu population that found itself in Pakistan had to make the difficult choice to migrate to India in order to preserve their lives and the lives of their loved ones. They left behind their ancestral homes, memories, and cherished possessions. They became refugees, seeking shelter and hope in the camps of India, and eventually, they forged a new life for themselves there.

As the years went by, circumstances led our family to embark on a journey to North America, where we found new beginnings, new opportunities, and a chance to build a life far from the shadows of the Partition.

My dear Beti, on this 75th Independence Day anniversary, I want you to remember the sacrifices made by countless souls like ours who endured the trials of the Partition with unwavering courage and strength. Let this day be a reminder that freedom comes at a great price, and it is our duty to preserve the values and principles that our nation stands for.

As you celebrate this historic day, always remember the stories of our ancestors, the sacrifices they made, and the resilience they showed. Let their legacy inspire you to be a responsible citizen, to cherish the unity in our diversity, and to promote peace and understanding.

With all my love,

Dad

August 14, 2022

Title: History, Memory, Art
Artist: Jaypreet Singh

Foreword

By Jaypreet Singh

I write this Foreword as the author's son, from another generation removed from the events of Partition, yet still carrying the silent burden of its memory. A strong, quiet desire to remember the tragedy that was inflicted and then passed down through our family informs these words. I wish to learn from and support my family's challenges and triumphs.

For example, my grandfather was a very successful writer, publishing over a dozen books and many newspaper articles in his time. He understood the power of information from an early age; this thirst to know the world and expand his horizons served him his entire life, and whatever he read, he memorized. This ability impressed and inspired me to follow in his footsteps, and I too became an avid reader. Now, his daughter, my mother, is publishing her first book to continue on with his legacy. With this contribution, I also aim to honor them and the untold millions affected by the events of 1947 and its aftermath. It is my first effort to become the third generation to echo their important work.

The image that introduces this foreword—a faded photograph of a family (my mother, grandfather, and grandmother) standing before a broken landscape—contains, of course, both a personal and historical document. Hidden in metaphor, however, is something much deeper: the inner landscape of the psychic blueprint of my immediate family. Look closely at the figures, smiling and vibrant, now subdued by the passage of time and the light-brown tint of memory. They are happy, yes, but the blood-red boundary line that shears the frame and cuts across the central figure, my mother and the author of this work, is no accident. It is the visible symbol of an ancestral trauma: the invisible wound of a great rupture that doesn't just run along the earth, it cuts through her soul and that of every generation that followed, including my own.

The background of a random pattern of cracked earth speaks directly to the trauma inflicted upon the people and the land. Moreover, its color also reflects the generally adopted term of "wheatish" skin tone for South Asians—a billion-plus strong shared identity defined by separation of Partition and the newly-formed nation-states replacing the British Raj. (The latter, of course, was also not above discrimination based on hue.) The age spots and darkened corners suggest that time, which should heal, can also obscure and deepen the shadows of unaddressed pain. This is the warning our story carries: one cannot build a successful future on a foundation of suppressed grief.

It is the silent anxiety, the quiet strength, and the unnamed pain that was passed down through the family. That is what I wished to address when designing this image.

I was privileged to grow up alongside the architects of survival: my grandfather and grandmother. They were loving, caring people whose presence in our family was a constant source of joy, humor, and stability. For a family whose world had once been shattered by chaos, my grandparents provided an unshakable rhythm. They lived with us during childhood: there was always warm food and even warmer smiles available when we came home. They ensured we spent time together, dedicating our weekends to visits to the park and Sunday school at the Gurdwara. I carry cherished memories of our time together: shared books, trips to places like Florida and the Kennedy Space Center, and their simple, profound commitment to family life.

Grandpa was a funny man, always speaking in rhymes—he had a unique one for every grandchild—and he loved to give us all special nicknames. As a child, I went by "JP," a short form for "Jaypreet," and he invented another phrase for me that kept these same initials: "Jammu and Punjab." No one else called me by that phrase and I would be tickled every time *Nanaji* (Grandpa) said those words out loud. As a published satirist, his love of wordplay knew no bounds: *Nanaji's* favorite nonsensical phrase was "I am right and you are left." How Grandma tolerated this, I will never know.

Despite his natural goofiness, his intellectual fire was shaped by some of the most respected and serious literary works of the 19th and 20th centuries. Like many of his time who could not afford their own literature, *Nanaji* would slip away to the local train station, reading left-behind newspapers and books, his imagination growing with every page. At the tender age of 14, he first read Irving Stone's *Lust for Life* and was so impressed that he memorized it, knowing the opportunities to come across the novel were scarce. Charles Dickens' *A Tale of Two Cities*, Tolstoy's *War and Peace*, and Ernest Hemingway's *Old Man and the Sea* were also among his favorites. *Nanaji* shared his passion and reverence for these authors and their masterpieces with me and instilled a love of literature that lit a fire that burns to this day. My own love of language and the published word feel like a natural extension of his genes into my own.

In fact, he scored so well in high school that his parents dreamed of sending him to England to study, a lofty achievement for a young man coming of age in 1950's Punjab. Unfortunately, the aftermath of 1947 left them unable to financially fulfill this dream. Nonetheless, he managed to soar academically at home and earned his PhD from the University of Punjab, a fine accomplishment for a man once relegated to reading books forgotten by hurried train passengers.

I learned, through their everyday choices, the kind of people my grandparents were— disciplined and organized, yet loving and caring. They built a secure world for us that was the opposite of the one they were forced to leave, a gift I am forever grateful for. May we, as their offspring, leave our next generation with the same love and kindness, no matter what life places before us.

Author's Statement

This book began not as a choice, but as a duty.

As the daughter of refugees from the 1947 Partition, I grew up in a "new" India, but my identity was forged by the unhealed wounds of the old one. The stories of my parents and grandparents were not just memories; they were the living, breathing explanation for the trauma, dislocation, and unspoken sorrow that defined our world.

My father, Balbir Singh Momi, was an accomplished writer, journalist, and researcher. He was also among the fortunate few who had the chance to return and visit his ancestral home on many occasions. He visited Pakistan seven times and slept in his own family home for six of them. But for us—and for so many grandchildren of survivors—we may never see the homes of our grandparents. Thanks to my father, we were able to visit my mother's home in the heart of Lahore, Pakistan. He wanted to bring his own parents back with him and decided the shock would be too much for them to bear. It was an emotional journey, a connection across borders and time.

The chapters are written as questions for the conversations I shared with my father. After each chapter, you will find a page titled '*Pause for a Moment's Reflection.*' This is a deliberate invitation to stop, observe your thoughts and the information put forward, and truly think about their implications before moving on to the next.

Lastly, I ask you, the reader, to remember this: refugees carry more than bags—they carry memories, longing, and hope. They are not criminals of circumstance, but survivors of it. They are hard-working people who never sit still, they feel discomfort in comfort. To be a refugee is not to be less than— it is to have lost, yet still dream. Judge not those who flee with empty hands—for they often carry the deepest stories, and the greatest strength.

SECTION 1:
HOW DID WE BECOME REFUGEES IN OUR OWN COUNTRY?

Chapter 1

What is the History of Pre-Partition India?

India's history is like a living canvas, stitched together over thousands of years with threads of civilizations, traditions, and empires. It is far more than a story of kings and conquests—it's the endurance of ordinary people, carrying their culture forward through every turmoil. That same spirit was alive in my parents, refugees of 1947's displacement, who carried with them both the trauma of loss and the unshakable pride of survival. Their stories shaped me as an artist; I see myself as one more thread woven into this vast fabric.

The journey begins with the Indus Valley Civilization, flourishing around 2500 BC in what is now Pakistan and northwest

India. The cities of Mohenjo-Daro and Harappa reveal a marvel of sophisticated urban planning. They were built with advanced drainage systems, organized trade, and were home to artisans who left behind a mysterious script we have yet to decipher.

Around 1500 BC, the Vedic Age dawned, bringing scriptures that became the accepted foundation of Hindu thought. Later, Buddhism and Jainism emerged, offering revolutionary spiritual paths that challenged old hierarchies and introduced profound new philosophies regarding the nature of life. Empires rose: Ashoka spread the message of compassion through Buddhism; the Gupta era celebrated knowledge, art, and invention, remembered as India's Golden Age.

The medieval era brought new voices and new blends. In the south, the Cholas built sky-reaching temples and commanded the seas. In the north, the Delhi Sultanate reshaped governance and culture, while Sufi mystics and Bhakti saints preached love and devotion beyond ritual. Persian poetry and architecture merged with local traditions, giving birth to something uniquely Indian.

This era also marked India's rise as a global trade hub. Its spices, fabrics, and jewels crossed oceans and deserts, carrying not just material goods but also philosophy, art, and ideas. Indian craftsmanship, especially in textiles and metalwork, became renowned across the known world.

And yet, India's history is not just about glory. It is about coexistence, devotion, and sometimes even division. Hinduism, Buddhism, Jainism, Islam, and Sikhism all found space to grow, layering their respective faith onto the land. That coexistence set the stage for what would later be torn apart by the splitting of South Asia. For me, that terrible event is not abstract history—it is my inheritance. My parents were forced from their homes to migrate to a new country, their survival etched into my very identity. That tension—between unity and division, between memory and loss—runs through my art. Every brushstroke is both an act of remembrance and renewal, a refusal to let stories be silenced.

As I carry these memories forward, my canvas becomes not just personal but historical, reaching back into the larger story of India itself. To understand the weight of my family's journey, I must also trace the forces that shaped the land we came from—the British Raj, the Partition, and the sizable shifts that altered identities and borders forever. The chapters ahead weave together fact and memory: the history of colonial rule, the trauma of 1947, and the stories of those who endured. By way of these intertwined narratives, I seek not only to honor the past but to uncover how its echoes still live in me, in my art, and in the generations that follow.

Pause for a Moment's Reflection

Chapter 2

What are the Historical and Core Beliefs of Hinduism?

The history we have just traced—from the planned cities of the Indus Valley to the diverse empires of the medieval era —was not built on a blank slate. It was consistently guided, challenged, and sustained by a profound spiritual and ethical framework. While empires rose and fell, the foundational beliefs of the subcontinent remained a constant force, deeply influencing everything from kingship and justice to social structure and the concept of duty. Recognizing this spiritual bedrock is essential, as the very principles that held diverse communities together for centuries were the same principles—like non-violence—that later fueled the peaceful freedom struggle against colonial rule. Before we go further into the political history of the British Raj and the trauma of division, we must first understand the ancient, unifying ideals that defined the soul of this land.

At the heart of Hinduism lie several core beliefs that shape its ethical and spiritual framework. Among the most fundamental is *ahimsa*, or non-violence. This principle calls for compassion and respect toward all living beings and is deeply embedded in Hindu scriptures. The philosophy of ahimsa was famously promoted by Mahatma Gandhi, who applied it to his dogma of non-violent resistance, inspiring movements for justice around the world.

Another key concept is *dharma*, which refers to the moral order and the duties individuals are expected to uphold. Dharma includes righteous behavior and ethical conduct, affirming actions that align with justice and fairness. Acts rooted in hatred, revenge, or violence are considered to violate dharma and disrupt social harmony.

Closely related is the belief in *karma*, the law of cause and effect. According to this teaching, every action has consequences, and negative deeds such as harboring malice or seeking revenge bring about harmful outcomes for the individual. Therefore, Hinduism generally discourages behavior driven by ill will or revenge.

Central to Hindu teachings is also the value of *forgiveness and compassion*. Many Hindu texts call for peaceful conflict resolution and encourage kindness even in difficult circumstances. This ethos holds the importance of maintaining harmony and treating others with empathy.

Integral to these beliefs is a profound *respect for life*. Hinduism encourages minimizing harm to others and living in harmony with all creatures. This respect manifests in practices that seek to protect and honor life, promoting peaceful cooperation.

While Hinduism is a diverse tradition made up of various schools of thought, each with unique views on scriptures, these traditions support non-violence, compassion, and right action. It is important to recognize that historical and cultural contexts have at times influenced different interpretations, and there have been episodes of conflict in history. However, these do not represent the core teachings of Hinduism.

Hindu ethos is fundamentally one of peace. As practices may vary, the core teachings examined in this chapter—from Dharma to Karma—all point toward a life that discourages hate, revenge, and killing, emphasizing instead understanding, forgiveness, and harmonious living. As the birthplace of peaceful religions like Hinduism, Buddhism, Jainism, and Sikhism, India has long been a beacon for those seeking peace. By embodying these values within our own communities, we can preserve this legacy of harmony and offer a powerful example for the world to follow.

Pause for a Moment's Reflection

Chapter 3

What are the Historical Foundations and Core Beliefs of Sikhism?

The ancient principles of Hinduism laid a spiritual and ethical bedrock in South Asia for thousands and thousands of years. Yet, the history of India is a story of continuing evolution, new wisdom, and profound reform. By the 15th century, during a time of social and religious turmoil, a new faith powerfully based in equality emerged from the very soil of Punjab, offering a revolutionary path forward: Sikhism.

Sikhism stands as one of India's most profound contributions to the world—a legacy of fairness, selfless service, and social justice. Founded by Guru Nanak Dev Ji in the 15th century,

Sikhism was guided by a lineage of Ten Human Gurus, beginning with Guru Nanak Dev Ji and ending with Guru Gobind Singh Ji. The faith established innovative principles rooted in the belief in one God and the oneness of all humankind, strongly rejecting the caste system and social hierarchy.

This commitment to equality led to the core of Sikh teaching, demanding an ethical life built around honest work (*Kirat Karō*), sharing with the community (*Vaṇḍ Chakkō*), and remembering God (*Nām Japnā*). This spiritual commitment became visible through social action, most notably through the concept of *Langar* (the free community kitchen). This tradition, started by the Gurus, requires everyone—regardless of caste, religion, wealth, or status—to sit together on the floor and share a vegetarian meal prepared and served by volunteers. Langar is a radical act of social leveling that promotes unity and human dignity. This commitment to selfless service (*Sēvā*) is a backbone of the Sikh ethos.

Adding to *Langar* is *Dasvandh*, or the spiritual practice of giving 10% (one-tenth) of one's earnings. This voluntary duty ensures funds are available for the maintenance of *Gurdwaras* (Sikh places of worships), for *Langar*, and for greater charitable projects.

The early Sikh Gurus translated these values into active defense of human rights. Guru Arjan Dev Ji (the fifth Guru) and Guru Tegh Bahadur Ji (the ninth Guru) played pivotal roles in defending the rights and freedoms of the people during periods of extreme Mughal suppression. Guru Arjan Dev Ji was executed by the Mughal Emperor Jahangir in 1606 for refusing to convert to Islam. Later, Guru Tegh Bahadur Ji opposed

Emperor Aurangzeb's policy of forced conversions against Hindus and was executed for his resistance. These acts were bold claims for religious freedom for all people.

The spiritual foundation laid by the first nine Gurus reached its peak with the tenth master, Guru Gobind Singh Ji (1666–1708). In a time of relentless opposition, Guru Gobind Singh Ji proved his mastery of military strategy, achieving notable victories in every major battle he personally led against the Mughal forces and hill rajas.

Facing ruthless religious repression from the later Mughal Empire, the Guru saw that spiritual belief and political defense had to join. In 1699, he performed the *Amrit Sanskar* (baptism ceremony) on the day of Vaisakhi, creating the Khalsa (the pure)—a formalized order of the Saint-Soldier (*Sant Sipahi*).

This key event began when Guru Gobind Singh Ji dramatically asked the crowd for five heads, a test of total dedication. Five men stepped forward, known today as the *Panj Pyare* (The Five Beloved Ones), who were baptized first. These individuals came from different backgrounds and castes, showing that all old social differences were wiped away to form a single, unified warrior class. The Guru then knelt before them, asking to be baptized by the *Panj Pyare* themselves, setting the ultimate example of humility and democracy within the faith.

The Khalsa were commanded to keep five articles of faith, known as the Five Ks (*Pañj Kakār*): Kesh (uncut hair), Kanga (comb), Kara (steel bracelet), Kirpan (ceremonial sword), and

Kacchera (cotton shorts). These articles provided a distinct and evident identity committed to discipline and defense.

Yet, despite his triumphs, Guru Gobind Singh Ji later experienced immense loss in the wars that followed, losing all four of his sons (the *Chaar Sahibzade*)—a supreme sacrifice that remains the most powerful example of commitment to the faith's ideals. The two elder sons, Baba Ajit Singh (age 18) and Baba Jujhar Singh (age 14), achieved heroic death fighting bravely in the Battle of Chamkaur.

The two younger sons, Baba Zorawar Singh (age 9) and Baba Fateh Singh (age 7), were captured alongside their grandmother, Mata Gujri Ji, and brutally bricked alive in a wall in Sirhind by the orders of the Mughal governor. Upon hearing of her grandsons' martyrdom, Mata Gujri Ji also passed away in captivity in the Thanda Burj (Cold Tower). This collective sacrifice of the four young princes and Mata Gujri Ji became a defining, sorrowful moment of courage that filled the Khalsa with a fierce determination.

Following these sacrifices, Guru Gobind Singh Ji formalized the Guru Granth Sahib Ji—the collection of sacred hymns from the Gurus and other saints—as the everlasting and spiritual Guru for all Sikhs. This act ensured that the focus of the faith would remain on the teachings and principles contained within the holy text, rather than on any single individual. Sikhs accept the Guru Granth Sahib Ji over any other authority or living person as the final word for all spiritual & worldly matters.

The text itself, now the Supreme Authority, is a powerful advocate for equality. Within the pages of the Guru Granth

Sahib Ji, the Gurus frequently adopted the voice of a woman (known as *Suhagan*, the devoted wife) to express the soul's yearning for union with the Divine, using the feminine perspective as the ideal spiritual seeker. This narrative choice underscores the inherent spiritual oneness embedded in the teachings, setting a clear example for social equality.

In South Asia, where women's standing was often greatly reduced, Sikh thought offered a strong, fresh voice for gender sameness. The Guru Granth Sahib openly rejects gender discrimination, stating that men and women are two sides of the same human coin. Guru Nanak Dev Ji famously asserted: "Why should we speak ill of her, who gives birth to kings?" The Gurus also eliminated the practice of *Sati* (widows self-immolating) and the isolation of *Purdah* (restricting women from public view), and actively encouraged women to lead gatherings and take part in all parts of life.

The Sikh spiritual torch was often carried by powerful female figures. Bibi Bhani Ji is respected for her selfless devotion and for being daughter of Guru Amar Das Ji, wife of Guru Raam Das Ji, mother of Guru Arjan Dev Ji, grandmother of Guru Hargobind Ji, great-grandmother of Guru Tegh Bahadur Ji, and great-great-grandmother of Guru Gobind Singh Ji. Mata Sahib Kaur was proclaimed the spiritual Mother of the Khalsa, symbolizing the spiritual energy infused into the Sikh nation. The most iconic example of military courage is Mai Bhago, a woman warrior who brought together 40 Sikh soldiers who had left their duty in 1705, leading them back into battle against the Mughals and herself fighting fiercely on the battlefield.

The principles of the Sikh faith have proven profoundly portable, inspiring a large-scale diaspora shaped by several distinct waves of migration. Even before the twentieth century, thousands of Sikh pioneers—many former soldiers or workers from the British Indian Army—settled in the United States and Canada, seeking work on farms and in lumber mills as subjects of the British Raj. These early settlers established the community's first foothold in North America. Today, while Sikhism remains deeply rooted in Punjab, it has become a truly global religion.

An estimated 25 million Sikhs live worldwide, making it the fifth-largest organized religion. Millions now form thriving communities across North America, the United Kingdom, Southeast Asia, and Australia. Wherever they have settled, Sikhs have upheld the principles of *Langar* and *Seva*, often serving as first responders in local and international crises. This cultural and spiritual resilience stands as living testimony to the community's enduring strength—and to the profound human story of South Asia itself.

Pause for a Moment's Reflection

Chapter 4

What is the History of the Mughals in India?

The Mughal Empire, founded in 1526 by Babur after his victory at the First Battle of Panipat, remains one of the most powerful dynasties in Indian history. For more than three centuries, the Mughals brought a degree of political unification, structural splendor, and cultural richness that left a permanent mark on the Indian subcontinent.

Beginning with Babur, who established the foundation of the empire, successive emperors such as Humayun, Akbar, Jahangir, Shah Jahan, and Aurangzeb expanded the reach of the Mughals across much of South Asia. Akbar the Great, whose reign lasted from 1556 to 1605, played a crucial role in consolidating imperial power. He established a centralized bureaucracy and implemented policies of religious tolerance, famously integrating Hindu Rajputs and other non-Muslims into key administrative and military positions. This inclusive governance model helped maintain stableness and fostered loyalty across a diverse and vast empire.

The empire's administrative framework relied heavily on a system that ranked officials and ensured loyalty through land grants and salaries. This military and civil service structure not only enabled effective influence but also integrated local rulers into the Mughal fold, reinforcing centralized control while allowing for regional flexibility.

Culturally, the Mughal period is often celebrated as a golden age of Indo-Islamic fusion. Persian was adopted as the court language, and literature flourished alongside other cultural pursuits such as calligraphy, miniature painting, music, and poetry. The arts benefited from imperial backing, and the resulting works reflected a fusion of Persian, Indian, and Central Asian styles. This cultural blend produced an aesthetic legacy that continues to influence Indian art and architecture today.

The architectural achievements of the Mughals are among their most visible and enduring contributions. Massive structures like the Red Fort, Fatehpur Sikri, Humayun's Tomb, and the Taj Mahal represent the brilliance and elegance of Mughal design. These buildings not only served political and ceremonial purposes but also symbolized the power and sophistication of the empire. Shah Jahan, in particular, is renowned for his support of architecture, with the Taj Mahal standing as a statement to both artistic mastery and personal devotion.

However, this grand empire began to fall following the death of Aurangzeb in 1707. His reign, marked by military campaigns and stricter religious policies, strained imperial resources and ignited resistance from various quarters, including the Marathas in the west and the Sikhs in the north. After his death, internal divisions and a growing regional desire for independence weakened the empire's central authority.

The rise of regional powers such as the Marathas and Sikhs, coupled with the invasion of European colonial forces—most notably the British East India Company—hurried the empire's decline. The Mughal court became increasingly symbolic, retaining a likeness of authority while actual power shifted to regional rulers and foreign powers.

Despite its eventual collapse, the Mughal Empire was more than a political dynasty. It was a cultural phenomenon that transformed the Indian subcontinent through its policies, aesthetics, and vision of governance. Its legacy endures not only in India's monuments and art forms but also in its language, cuisine, and intellectual outlook. The story of the Mughals is one of royalty and decline, unity and diversity, conquest and cultural fusion—an enduring chapter in the long and complex history of India.

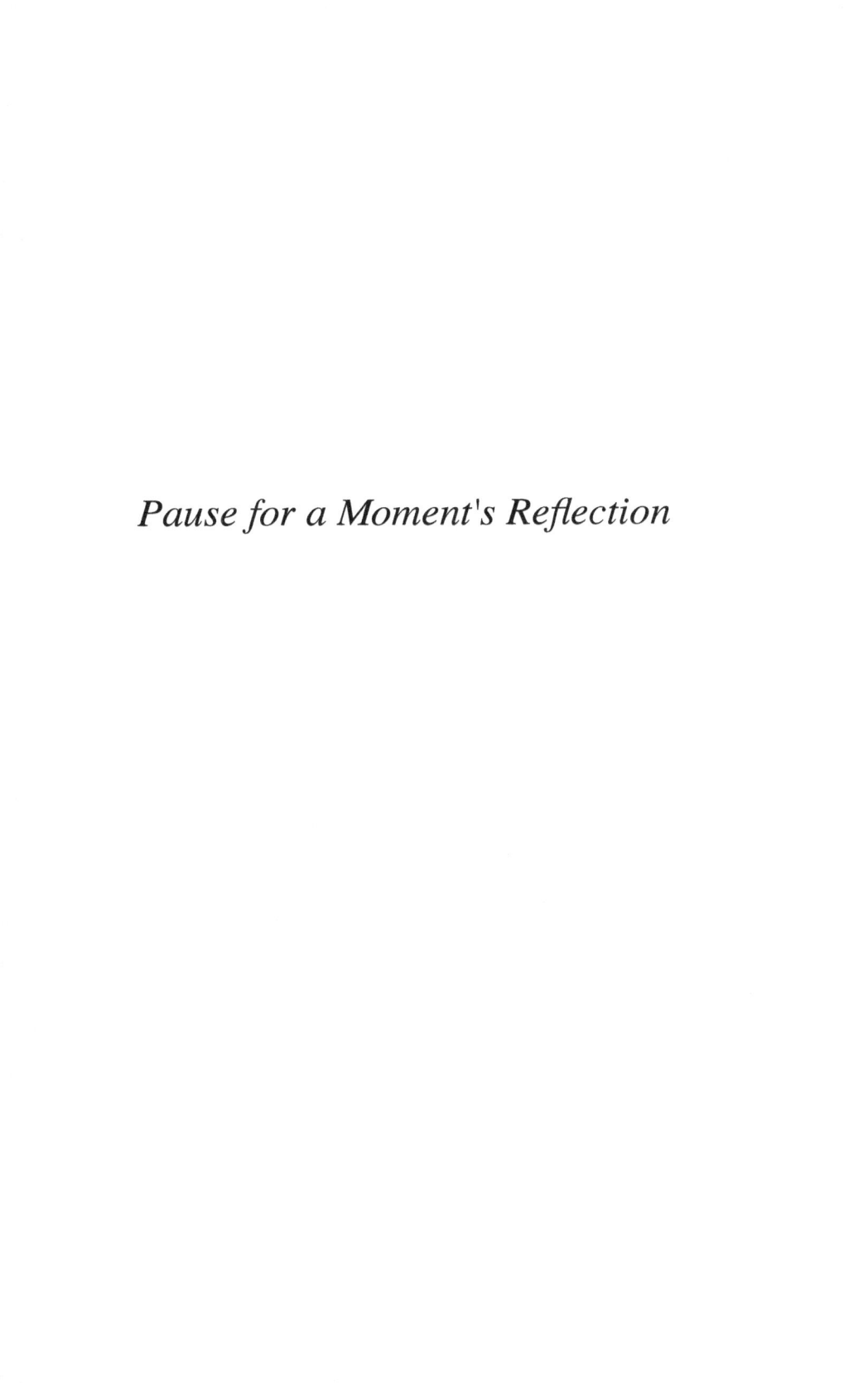

Pause for a Moment's Reflection

Chapter 5

What was the History of the British in India?

British involvement in India began as a corporate venture. In the 1600s, the East India Company arrived with a royal charter and a simple goal: trade. What started first as a commercial experiment in spices and silk gradually transformed into a force of total imperial domination, reshaping South Asia's economic and cultural landscapes in devastating ways.

The Company established trading posts in key coastal cities including Surat, Madras, Bombay, and Calcutta. These ports quickly became centers of immense wealth and footholds for greater influence. The pivotal Battle of Plassey in 1757 marked the turning point, as Robert Clive's victory over the Nawab of Bengal opened the door to political control over one of India's wealthiest regions. Following the Battle of Buxar in 1764, the Company acquired the *Diwani* rights—the legal authority to collect tax revenues directly from the people. From that moment, the Company stopped being guests and became the official landlords of the eastern provinces, extracting vast fortunes to ship back to London.

By the early 19th century, this private corporation had extended its control over vast parts of the Indian subcontinent. The Company systematically dismantled India's traditional economy to serve British markets. They restructured agriculture to produce cash crops like indigo, cotton, and opium instead of food grains, leading to severe and recurring famines. Indigenous industries, especially the world-renowned textile looms of Bengal, were systematically destroyed to eliminate competition for British factories, turning a land of producers into a market of consumers.

The Indian Rebellion of 1857—often called the First War of Independence—erupted as a direct challenge to this corporate exploitation. Rooted in widespread discontent among soldiers and civilians alike, the uprising exposed the brutality of Company rule. Although the rebellion was suppressed, it forced the British Crown to dissolve the Company and assume direct control, taking India from a corporate asset to an imperial jewel.

Under this new era, India witnessed a rapid transformation of its inner networks. The British constructed massive railway connections, telegraph systems, and postal services, alongside extensive irrigation canals in Punjab. Yet, these modernizations were designed to extract raw materials for the Industrial Revolution and move troops quickly, rather than to benefit the local population. India's wealth was taken entirely for imperial benefit, often to the profound disservice of local communities.

This colonial legacy is dual-edged. On one hand, it introduced modern institutions, English education, and global trade networks that persist today. On the other, it left deep economic scars, disrupted traditional ways of life, and sowed divisions that would later manifest in communal tensions. The British did not just rule India; they fundamentally altered its destiny. By the time they departed in 1947, they left behind a nation that was modernized yet deprived, connected yet divided. The history of British India is a tale of how unchecked economic power consumed an entire civilization, leaving behind a legacy that takes centuries to heal.

Pause for a Moment's Reflection

Chapter 6

When was the British Raj (Colonial Rule) in India?

The British Raj, from 1858 to 1947, marked the era of direct imperial rule by the British Crown. This period began immediately after the 1857 Rebellion, a defining moment that ended the East India Company's reign. Queen Victoria was declared the Empress of India in 1876, symbolizing the total merger of India into the British Empire.

The Raj would go on to fundamentally reshape India's political institutions, economic structures, and cultural identities. As an artist and story-teller of historical trauma and triumph, revisiting this colonial episode is essential to understanding the roots of division, displacement, and resilience.

The Raj imposed a highly centralized official system. At its peak stood the Viceroy, appointed by London, who ruled with absolute authority. Below him, districts were managed by British collectors and judges who exercised tremendous power over millions, often serving as judge, jury, and tax collector in a single role. The country was divided between territories governed directly by British officials and "princely states" ruled by Indian monarchs who operated under strict British monitoring. This dual system allowed the British to maintain control with relatively few officials by co-opting local elites to enforce their will.

Racial hierarchy was the hallmark of the Raj. Indians were systematically excluded from high positions of authority and subjected to prejudiced laws. Education systems prioritized British values and the English language, often dismissing Indian knowledge as lesser. Socially, the British maintained a rigid distance, living in separate quarters and creating a "ruling caste" that demanded inferiority, often barring Indians from elite clubs. To maintain control over this vast population, the administration codified the policy of "divide and rule" through the Morley-Minto Reforms of 1909, which introduced separate electorates based on religion, formalizing communal division.

Despite this oppressive system, organized resistance took root. The formation of the Indian National Congress in 1885 created the first unified political platform for Indian voices. Over time, this movement grew in strength and strategy. Leaders like Bal Gangadhar Tilak, Jawaharlal Nehru, and Master Tara Singh played crucial roles in mobilizing the masses. The 1919 Jallianwala Bagh massacre in Amritsar further hardened national resolve, stripping the Empire of its moral mask. This outrage deepened with the 1928 Simon Commission, where the death of Punjabi leader Lala Lajpat Rai ignited a revolutionary fire in the youth.

Mahatma Gandhi later transformed this national anger into a disciplined struggle by introducing the philosophy of *Satyagraha*—nonviolent resistance and civil disobedience. His mass mobilization campaigns, such as the Salt March and the Quit India Movement, paralyzed the colonial administration and galvanized international support for the Indian cause. His approach brought together people across religions, languages, and regions in a collective demand for *Swaraj* (self-rule).

World War II dealt the final blow to the Raj. Britain, exhausted by the war and facing revolts within the Indian military, realized it could no longer hold South Asia by force. The decision to leave was made, but the exit was devastating. The demand for a separate Muslim homeland, formalized in the 1940 Lahore Resolution, had made unity impossible. The British departure in 1947 was accompanied by the violent splitting of the land into India and Pakistan—a decision driven by colonial tactics that had deepened religious tensions for decades.

The legacy of the British Raj is complex. While it created the political framework of modern India, including its parliamentary democracy and legal system, its primary legacy remains one of extraction and division. The policies carried out over nearly a century disrupted India's cultural unity and sowed seeds of unrest that still endure in South Asia. As India continues to reflect on its past, the story of the Raj serves as a powerful reminder of resistance—the enduring spirit of a people who fought for ninety years to reclaim their identity, people who fought for ninety years to reclaim their identity, their land, and their freedom. It stands as a statement to the determined will of a nation that refused to be silenced.

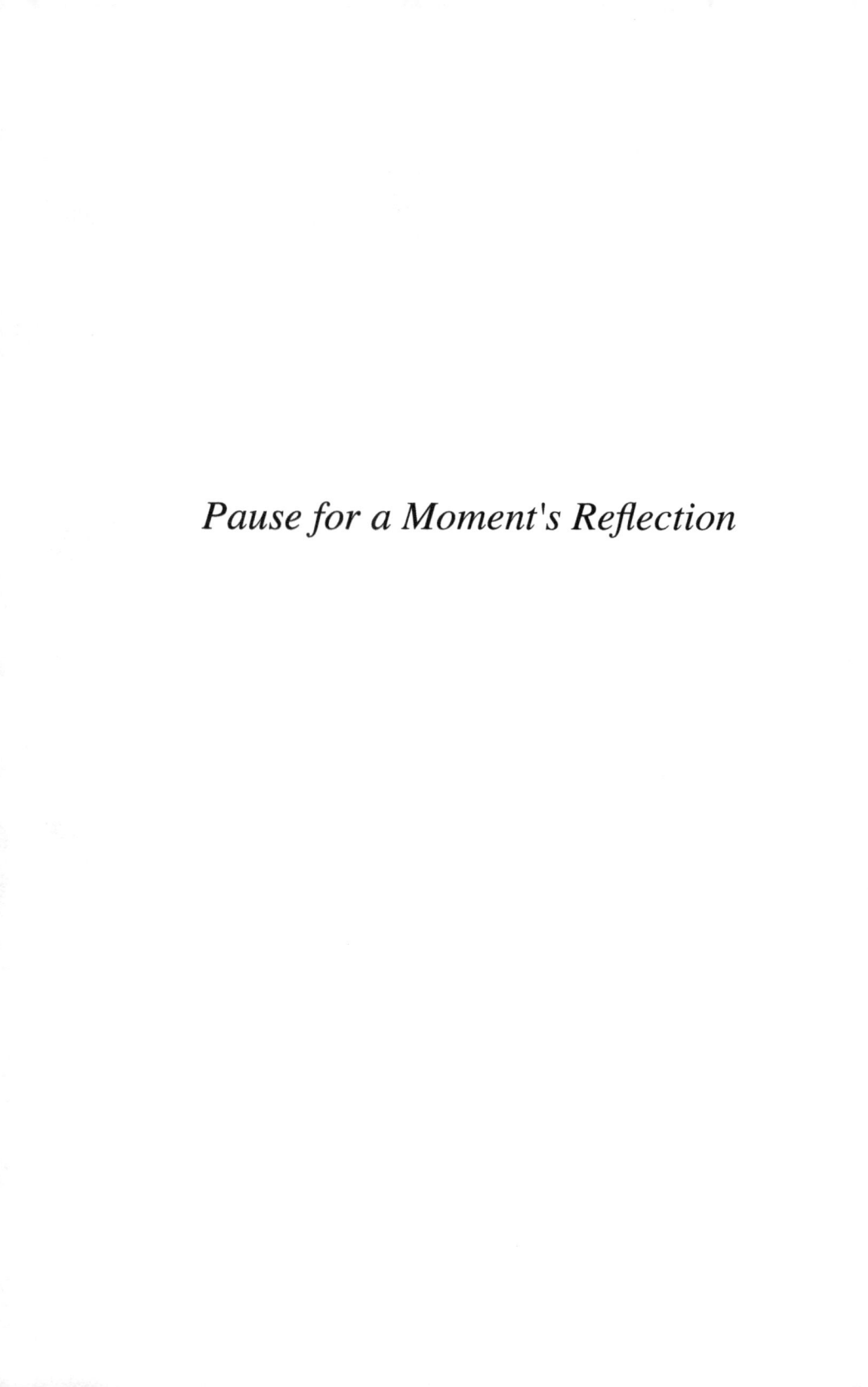

Pause for a Moment's Reflection

Chapter 7

Divide and Rule: Churchill's Strategy of Power and Manipulation?

The "divide and rule" strategy—also known as "divide and conquer"—has long been used in political and social contexts to weaken opposition and maintain control. By fostering divisions within a population, those in power are able to prevent unified resistance and maintain dominance. This approach thrives on taking advantage of existing tensions—religious, cultural, ethnic, or class-based—or by creating new ones where none previously existed.

In colonial India, the British used this tactic with surgical precision. One of the most significant manifestations of this policy was their intentional empowerment of the Muslim League while at the same time diminishing the influence of the Indian National Congress. By cultivating favor with Muslim League leaders, especially M.A. Jinnah, the British deepened the divide between India's Hindu and Muslim populations. These decisions widened communal rifts and set the stage for the devastating division of India in 1947.

This approach to leadership—fostering separation rather than unity—is captured in a stark contrast: *There are only two ways to lead: you either divide and conquer, or you build and unite.* The British colonial strategy clearly chose the former, and India paid the price.

Winston Churchill, a towering figure in British political history, demonstrated the cruel arrogance that often underpinned colonial attitudes. Beyond his strong opposition to Indian independence, his policies resulted in one of the greatest humanitarian disasters of the 20th century. During the Bengal Famine of 1943, British wartime policies regarding grain storage and distribution, combined with Churchill's refusal to divert necessary food aid, led to the deaths of an estimated 2 to 3 million people. This tragedy reveals the low value the colonial administration placed on Indian lives.

Churchill is said to have remarked, "If independence is granted to India, power will go to the hands of rascals...; all Indian leaders will be of low caliber and men of straw. They will have sweet tongues and silly hearts. They will fight amongst themselves for power..."

His contempt for India's emerging leadership was especially evident in his comments about Gandhi and Nehru. Gandhi, he sneered, was a "Middle Temple lawyer" posing as a "half-naked fakir," while Nehru was dismissed as a "Communist, revolutionary" and one of the enemies "of the British connection with India."

Even Gandhi's assassination, a massive moment in Indian history, failed to stir genuine compassion from Churchill. In the House of Commons, he referred to it as "an awful tragedy," but quickly shifted focus to the communal butchery it symbolized, noting that "at least 400,000 men and women have slaughtered each other in the Punjab alone."

The legacy of divide and rule in India did not end with Independence. It left behind deep divisions—collective, political, and psychological—that continue to challenge South Asia. By understanding how colonial powers manipulated these ruptures, we can begin to confront the consequences of division and seek new paths toward unity, justice, and healing.

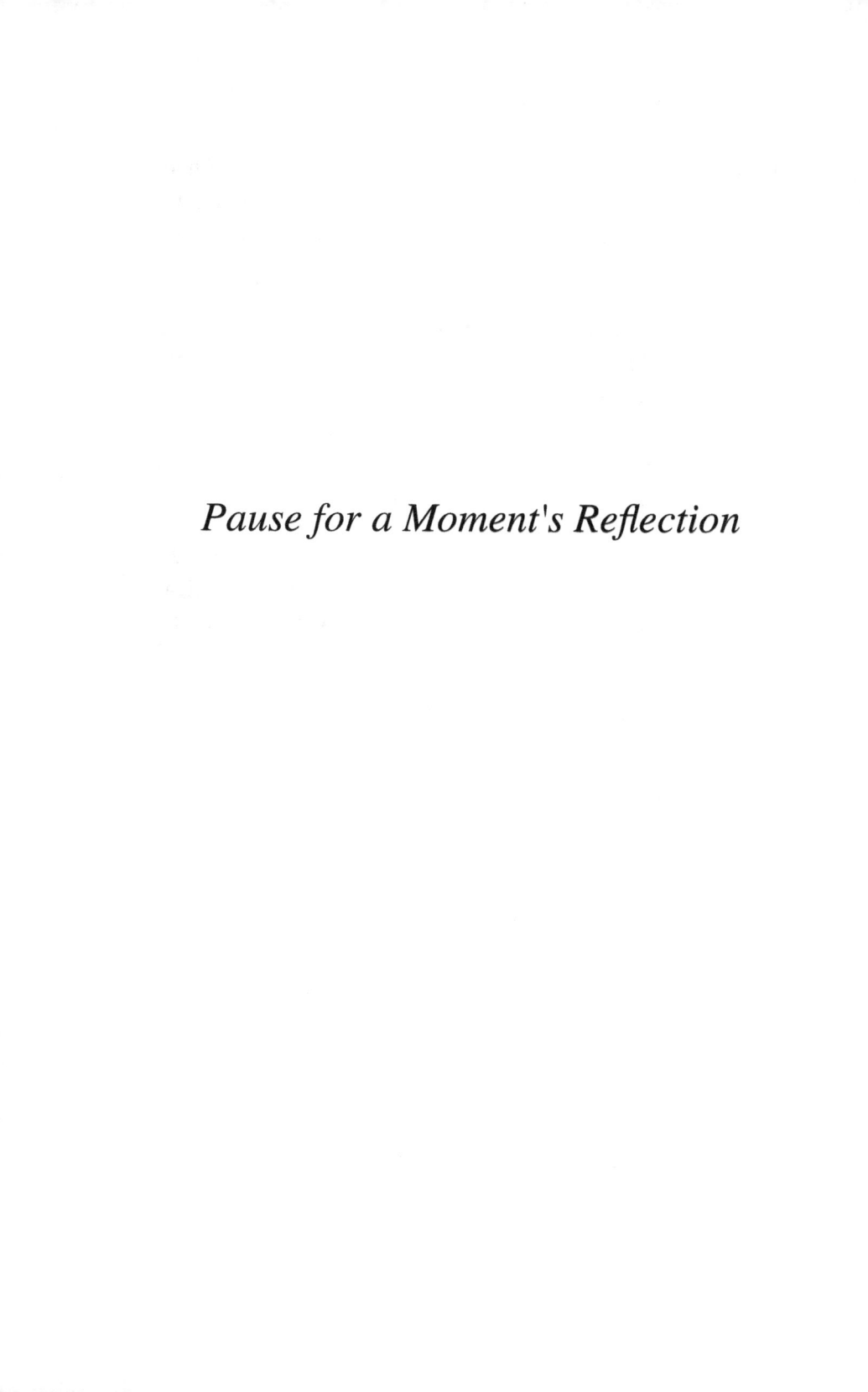

Pause for a Moment's Reflection

Chapter 8

What is the History of Pre-Partition Punjab?

Punjab, whose name means "Land of Five Rivers" (Persian: *panj* 'five' + *āb* 'water'), is a historically vital region in South Asia. Its fertile plains, irrigated by the Beas, Sutlej, Raavi, Chenab, and Jhelum rivers, made it a highly prized agricultural heartland and a crucial trade route for thousands of years. It served as the main gateway to South Asia, seeing the passage of invaders and great empires—from Alexander the Great to the Mughals. This constant role as a crossroads resulted in a rich, blended culture, heavily influenced by Persian, Central Asian, and local Indian traditions.

The land's history stretches back to the very beginning of Indian history. The lands of historical Punjab, including modern-day Haryana, are the birthplace of the Vedic period, where the ancient hymns of the Rig Veda were first collected. Later, during the time of extensive trade, Punjab served a critical function as the western gateway and a major junction on the Silk Road, helping trade and the exchange of goods, ideas, and religions between the Indian subcontinent, Persia, and Central Asia for centuries. The final, unified expression of this rich, blended culture was the Sikh Empire, established by Maharaja Ranjit Singh in the late 18th century. This era of indigenous rule was the last time Punjab existed as a unified, independent state before the British conquest fundamentally changed the region's political and social structure, setting the definitive stage for the colonial era.

Before the traumatic events of 1947, Punjab stood as an energized and culturally rich province in the Indian subcontinent and was both agriculturally prosperous and spiritually vibrant. It was home to an assortment of faiths, including Sikhs, Muslims, Hindus, and others, living in shared spaces marked by diverse traditions and a unity in language.

Punjab before Independence was unique in its interwoven religious and cultural life. The 1941 census revealed a population that was roughly 53% Muslim, 30% Hindu, and 14% Sikh. Despite differences in faith, Punjabis shared language, customs, festivals, dress, and even places of worship. In rural areas, it was common for communities to participate in each other's celebrations—*melas* and *baisakhis*—reflecting the deeply intermixed culture. Sufi shrines and Sikh gurudwaras stood not as symbols of separation but as spaces of overlapping regard. The Punjabi language itself, spoken across religious communities, served as a cultural bridge.

Punjab was one of British India's most economically developed provinces due to the vast canal irrigation systems constructed under colonial rule. The so-called Canal Colonies in Western Punjab, established in the late 19th and early 20th centuries, transformed the rural economy. However, this development also reinforced landownership orders. Wealthier Muslim landlords and Sikh peasant *zamindars* gained from the new system, while landless laborers and small farmers faced growing inequalities.

British colonial rule in Punjab was marked by both development and deepening communal divides. The British employed a strategy of divide and rule, especially after the 1857 rebellion. Communal representation in assemblies and government jobs was increasingly based on religion, which sowed seeds of mistrust. In the early 20th century, Punjab became a hotbed of political activism. The Ghadar Movement, led by Punjabi emigrants from North America between 1913 and 1917, aimed to overthrow British rule through armed revolution. The Jallianwala Bagh Massacre in 1919, in which hundreds of peaceful protestors were killed in Amritsar, increased anti-colonial sentiment.

The horror of Jallianwala Bagh was immediately and deeply felt across the province, marking a point of no return in the relationship between the British and the people of Punjab. The cold-blooded nature of the attack—where General Dyer ordered his troops to fire on unarmed men, women, and children trapped in a walled garden—destroyed any remaining illusion of the British Empire as a compassionate or civilizing force. It galvanized political opinion, not just against the *policy* of British rule, but against the very *morality* of foreign control. This atrocity instantly turned countless moderate Punjabis into dedicated nationalists, setting a far more aggressive tone for the coming political resistance. *My own paternal grandfather, Bhagat Singh, and his brother, Santa Singh, were among the freedom fighters who protested the massacre and were later arrested—a legacy of courage and sacrifice that is the source of immense pride for our family today.*

The massacre also heightened the importance of Amritsar—the spiritual capital for Sikhs and a major commercial hub—as a central site of political confrontation. In the years that followed, this collective trauma fueled a wave of militant and non-violent resistance movements across the province, from the Akali Movement for gurdwara reform to the growing influence of the Indian National Congress. For the Sikhs, the event was especially significant as it occurred near the Golden Temple, reinforcing the belief that their community's fate was linked to the struggle for political self-determination in the region. This increased political mobilization, though initially anti-colonial, would worsen the communal fault lines the British had been cultivating.

By exposing the brutality of colonial administration, Jallianwala Bagh served as a tragic prelude to the violence of 1947. The slaughter shattered Punjab's sense of political stability and collective security. Yet, once the shared anti-colonial focus began to break in the 1930s and 40s, the memory of state-authorized violence—and the failure of different communities to find a path forward—contributed to an atmosphere where communal mistrust and radical action became dangerously normalized. This set the stage for the horrific breakdown of law and order that accompanied the quick departure of the British authorities.

By the 1930s and 1940s, Punjab's political landscape was divided among the Unionist Party, the Muslim League, the Indian National Congress, and the Akali Dal, each representing different visions of Punjab's future. The idea of a separate Muslim homeland—Pakistan—gained ground in the 1940s. The Lahore Resolution of 1940, passed by the Muslim League, expressly called for independent Muslim-majority states. Punjab, with its Muslim majority and deeply interwoven communities, suddenly became a contested space.

As British withdrawal loomed, Punjab was torn between competing nationalist agendas. The 1946 territorial elections, which saw a sweeping victory for the Muslim League among the Muslim voting public, signaled that the fragile communal agreements were breaking down. In the months leading up to August 1947, Punjab descended into chaos. What had once been shared neighborhoods and marketplaces became battlegrounds. Massacres, abductions, and village burnings marked the land.

Pre-Partition Punjab was a region of richness—culturally, spiritually, and economically. Remembering it is essential not just for understanding the trauma of 1947 but for honoring a time when diversity thrived. Its memory is a reminder of what was lost—and what could be possible again.

Pause for a Moment's Reflection

Chapter 9

Who was Maharaja Ranjit Singh?

Maharaja Ranjit Singh, remembered as the "Lion of Punjab," was a visionary leader who carved out a powerful and unified Sikh Empire during one of the most troubled periods in Indian history. Born on November 13, 1780, in Gujranwala—now part of Pakistan—he came into the world during a time of great political instability. The once-mighty Mughal Empire was declining, and Punjab was split into twelve Sikh Misls. Ranjit Singh belonged to the Sukerchakia Misl and was only a child when he lost his father, Mahan Singh. By the age of 18, he rose to leadership—a young warrior with a sharp mind and a fierce spirit.

From the very beginning of his rule, Ranjit Singh demonstrated extraordinary military and tactical foresight. He dreamt of a united Punjab, free from the internal strife and external threats that had long plagued the region. Through a combination of battlefield insight and careful diplomacy, he began consolidating power by bringing various Sikh Misls under his leadership. His capture of Lahore in 1799, which he declared the capital of his empire by 1805, marked a turning point in Punjab's history. From this stronghold, he launched military campaigns that would ultimately expand his rule to include much of present-day Punjab, Haryana, Himachal Pradesh, and Jammu and Kashmir.

What made Maharaja Ranjit Singh's reign especially remarkable was not just the scale of his conquests but the character of his rule. His court was known for its religious diversity and cultural sophistication. Though a devout Sikh, he upheld a policy of religious tolerance that was rare for the time. Under his rule, Hindus, Muslims, and Sikhs all worshipped freely, and positions of power were awarded based on merit rather than faith. Mosques were restored, temples were protected, and gurdwaras flourished. His secular approach to governance won him respect from all communities and helped foster a sense of shared identity across the diverse regions of his empire.

Beyond military and religious affairs, Maharaja Ranjit Singh was a reformer who recognized the importance of modernization. He developed a centralized administrative system, reorganized tax collection, and encouraged trade and industry. His army was among the most disciplined and modern in South Asia, incorporating European military techniques and even employing European officers to train his soldiers. These advancements brought both stability and prosperity to Punjab during his reign, earning him admiration not just within India but from foreign observers as well.

Ranjit Singh also understood the necessity of navigating the growing power of the British East India Company. Rather than engage in premature conflict, he maintained diplomatic ties with the British, skillfully balancing cooperation with sovereignty. His government signed the Treaty of Amritsar, which formalized relations between his empire and the British, securing peace during his lifetime. However, this peace would not last beyond his death.

When Ranjit Singh passed away on June 27, 1839, in Lahore, the empire he had built began to unravel. Succession disputes and weakened leadership led to internal discord. Within a decade, the Sikh Empire, once a symbol of unity and strength, crumbled under the pressure of British imperial growth. Following the Second Anglo-Sikh War, the British annexed Punjab in 1849, bringing an end to the independent Sikh state.

Despite the fall of his empire, Maharaja Ranjit Singh remains one of the most celebrated rulers in Indian history. He is remembered not only as a fierce warrior and empire-builder but also as a just ruler, a unifier, and a symbol of Sikh pride. His contributions to Punjab's political and cultural landscape continue to be felt today. Statues, stories, and songs across India and the Sikh diaspora pay tribute to his enduring legacy—a leader who, in a deeply divided time, showed what it meant to lead with strength, fairness, and vision.

Pause for a Moment's Reflection

Chapter 10

Who was Duleep Singh?

After the passing of Maharaja Ranjit Singh, the great Sikh Empire he had built with brilliance and resolve began to fall. It wasn't just a political decline—it was the slow undoing of an identity. At the heart of this collapse emerged the life of his youngest son, Maharaja Duleep Singh—a life marked by exile, loss, and the deep longing for a homeland he was never allowed to truly know.

Duleep Singh was born on September 6, 1838, in Lahore to Maharaja Ranjit Singh and Maharani Jind Kaur. Just ten months old when his father died, he was thrown into the turbulence of court plots, power struggles, and British interference. At the age of five, he was declared the Maharaja of Punjab, a crown that weighed heavily on a child surrounded by adults eager to control him. His mother, Jind Kaur, served as regent, fiercely protective of his rights and legacy, but the British saw her strength as a threat. She was soon removed and exiled, and the young king was taken into British custody.

In 1849, after the Second Anglo-Sikh War, the British annexed Punjab and forced the ten-year-old Duleep Singh to sign away his empire and the famed Koh-i-Noor diamond. Isolated from his mother, religion, and homeland, he was sent to live under the guardianship of a British officer, Dr. John Login, in Fatehgarh. Under British care, he was raised as a Christian and taught to think and live like an English gentleman. At fifteen, he was baptized and sent to England, where he would spend most of his life.

In England, Duleep Singh became a favorite of Queen Victoria and was welcomed by British high society with fascination—as both royalty and an exotic novelty. He was given estates and wealth, including his own estate in Suffolk, where he lived a lavish lifestyle, hosting hunting parties and raising his family.

In 1864, Duleep Singh married Bamba Müller, the daughter of a German merchant and an Ethiopian woman. Their union was both a love story and a quiet act of dignity by a displaced ruler who longed to build something of his own. Together, they had six children—three sons and three daughters. Among them, Princess Sophia Duleep Singh would later become a prominent figure in the British women's rights movement, fighting for their right to vote. She carried forward her father's legacy of resistance, though by a very different path.

Despite the wealth and the appearances of comfort, Duleep Singh was restless. After reuniting with his mother in England in 1861—just two years before her death—he began to question everything he had been taught. Her return awakened in him the spiritual memory of his Sikh heritage, and he slowly began to reclaim his identity. In the 1880s, he left Christianity and sought to return to Sikhism. He also started plotting to reclaim his throne, reaching out to European powers and Indian revolutionaries with dreams of raising an army and marching back to Punjab.

The British government, however, was watching closely. They blocked his travel plans, seized his mail, and did everything to prevent him from returning to India. His dream of reclaiming Punjab remained unfulfilled. By the end of his life, Duleep Singh was alone, estranged from his children, and living in exile in Paris, where he died on October 22, 1893. He was just fifty-five years old.

His daughters, especially Sophia, carried forward his name with quiet dignity. Though raised in England, Sophia Duleep Singh identified deeply with her Indian heritage and the injustices of colonialism. She stood on the front lines of the women's voting movement in the UK, risking arrest and social rejection. Though her father's crown had been stolen, she wore his courage like armor.

The story of Maharaja Duleep Singh is one of both tragedy and great dignity. A prince turned pawn of empire, his life was shaped by loss—of homeland, of identity, and of family. But it was also shaped by an unbreakable longing to return, to remember, and to reclaim. He was not just the last Maharaja of Punjab; he was the living symbol of a people's fractured history.

Through his daughters, especially Princess Sophia, and the memory of his struggle, Duleep Singh remains an enduring figure in Sikh and Indian consciousness. His life stands as a powerful reminder of how colonialism didn't just conquer land, it also stole lineage, language, and the right to remember.

The exile and death of Maharaja Duleep Singh was the first tragedy, a dark omen that finalized the loss of Sikh power and independence in the 19th century. Yet, this loss was made absolute a century later, not by an invading army, but by a flawed political act. The failure of the new Indian leadership to preserve the unity of the land also became a profound moral failure for the Sikh community. Congress leaders promised a separate state to the Sikhs, only to go back on their word. This political failure, coupled with the drawing of the border directly through the Sikh heartland of Punjab, would lead to the total collapse of Sikh independence and a defining tragedy of the 20th century.

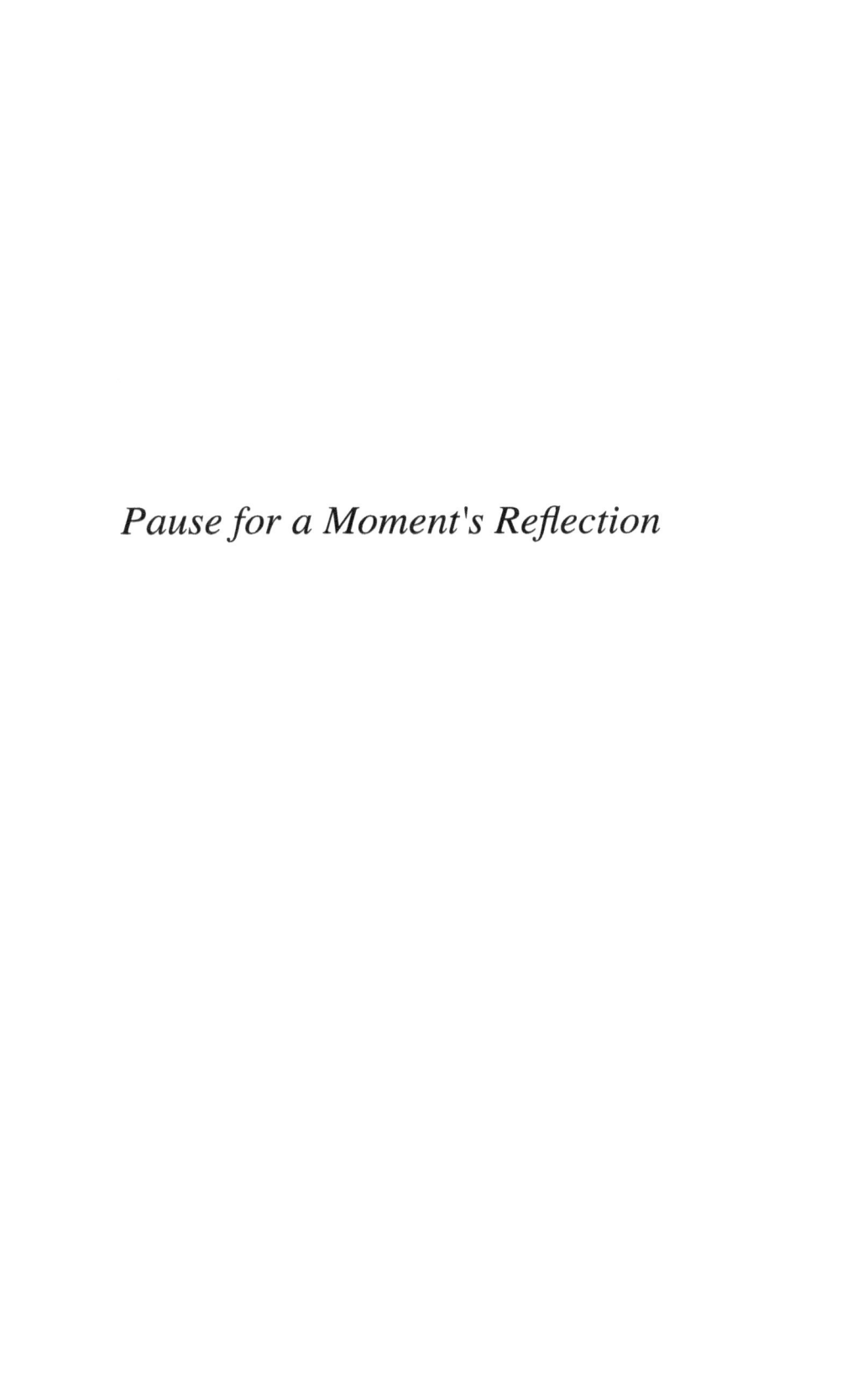

Pause for a Moment's Reflection

Chapter 11

Partition: A Mess Created by Three Lawyers?

The split of India and Pakistan was a massive human disaster. It unleashed a wave of terrible violence, mass migration, and ethnic cleansing that was hard to imagine. While many factors caused this disaster—including colonial tactics to divide and rule and deep religious conflicts—my father once made a strong case that the *chaos* of Partition was largely created by the choices and stubborn legal thinking of three key leaders, all of whom shared the same background: they were all lawyers. Jawaharlal Nehru, Muhammad Ali Jinnah, and Mahatma Gandhi each made choices, based on their own political goals, that ultimately guaranteed the division would be fast, brutal, and badly managed.

Muhammad Ali Jinnah, who trained as a lawyer in England, brought the demanding, argumentative style of the courtroom to the political talks. His main role in creating the mess was his firm, non-negotiable demand for a separate Muslim country: Pakistan.

Jinnah's relentless pursuit of this state effectively eliminated any possibility of a self-governing Sikh state from the negotiating table. Jinnah used his legal skill to firmly establish the Two-Nation Theory—the idea that Hindus and Muslims were two completely different peoples who could not live together peacefully in one country. This theory inherently excluded the Sikhs as a group with their own political demands. Because his lawyer's mindset meant he saw politics as a negotiation where any compromise was a failure, he refused various unity plans, like the Cabinet Mission Plan, because they did not give the total, independent country he felt his "client" (the Muslim community) deserved.

The chaos grew worse because of his demand for "Pakistan or perishing" and his call for "Direct Action Day" in August 1946. This political move, meant to show the strength of his demand, quickly exploded into wide-scale religious violence, setting the stage for the chaotic nature of the actual split. Jinnah's focused drive for a clear and legal separation created a problem that no amount of practical planning could ever fix.

Jawaharlal Nehru, also a Western-educated lawyer, was the main voice of the powerful Indian National Congress and was chosen to lead the new Indian state. His main role in the mess was his quick agreement to splitting the countries and his failure to properly plan how the changeover would be handled.

Nehru and the Congress leaders grew tired of the political deadlock and the quickly worsening violence between communities. Their focus on practical outcomes—which critics call an impatience for power—made them accept the British schedule for handing over power, a timeline that Lord Mountbatten, sped up dangerously. Nehru famously dismissed the idea of a slow, carefully planned transfer of power.

This rush to take control meant the realistic work of separating a civilization—dividing armies, police, money, train systems, and millions of people—was dangerously ignored. The decision to accept the splitting of Punjab and Bengal, which cut through whole communities and instantly left millions trapped on the "wrong" side of a new border, was a terrible political error made under his command. Nehru focused on the legal and political transfer, not the human details, ensuring that when the dividing line was drawn, the people were entirely defenseless.

Mahatma Gandhi, who trained as a lawyer in London and South Africa, approached politics not through law books, but through the moral power of *Satyagraha* (non-violent resistance). His role in the mess was his failure to find a working political solution and his decision to mostly step away from the talks.

Gandhi viewed Partition as a spiritual and personal disaster, famously saying that India would be divided "over my dead body." However, by 1947, his moral authority, though still powerful among the common people, had weakened among the top political figures, including his own followers, Nehru and Vallabhbhai Patel.

Gandhi's refusal to deal with the political reality of Jinnah's demands, and his insistence on an idealized, non-violent, unified India, left him sidelined in the final months. He could not convince the Muslim League to drop their demand for separation, nor could he convince his own party to reject the quick transfer of power. His principled decision to withdraw from the main bargaining meant that the chaos was ultimately delivered by the political leaders and the departing British, without the steady influence of the one figure whose moral standing might have demanded a gentler process.

The three lawyers, for all their different methods—Jinnah's legal fight for a separate state, Nehru's functional move for power, and Gandhi's moral vision—all failed to grasp the explosive reality they were dealing with. The chaos of Partition was the direct result of a political agreement being forced through without any serious thought or plan for human safety. The lawyers delivered the official documents for the division, but they left the people to pay the ultimate cost.

Pause for a Moment's Reflection

Chapter 12

How Were the India-Pakistan Borders Drawn?

The process of physically carving the boundary that would slice British India into two separate nations was not a carefully considered diplomatic effort, but a rushed, purely technical affair with devastating results. The responsibility fell to Sir Cyril Radcliffe, a British lawyer who had never previously stepped foot in India. Arriving on July 8, 1947, with zero experience of South Asia's complex social fabric, Radcliffe was handed an impossible mandate: to carve a locational line through a region of deep cultural, economic, and agricultural complexity in merely five weeks. He would essentially decide the fate of millions from the isolation of a Delhi bungalow, largely detached from the dusty, chaotic reality on the ground, ultimately destroying his own papers to leave no record of his reasoning.

Radcliffe's instructions were to divide the map roughly by faith—assigning Muslim-majority areas to Pakistan and Hindu-majority areas to India. On paper, this seemed like a simple administrative task. In reality, it was a surgical disaster. The communities of South Asia did not live in neat, separate blocks; they were woven together like fabric. Entire districts in Punjab and Bengal were a patchwork of faiths. Punjab, specifically, was an intricate web of Sikh, Muslim, and Hindu villages that relied on a shared, unified irrigation system—the finest in the British Empire.

Radcliffe was instructed to consider "other factors" beyond religion, a hazy order that essentially meant deciding who would control the vital ducts of the region—the massive canal headworks, railway lines, and power grids. These decisions would determine economic survival for millions. For the Sikhs, the line was especially a disaster, slicing through their heartland and leaving sacred shrines like *Nankana Sahib* (Guru Nanak Dev Ji's birthplace) on one side and their agricultural lands on the other. These life-altering judgments were made in isolation, using outdated maps and census data, without visiting the land in question to see the human cost.

Working against a ticking clock and rising communal tensions, he finalized the boundaries for East and West Pakistan and the Indian Union. The resulting "Radcliffe Line" was not announced until August 17, 1947—two days after Independence had been declared. This distinct delay was perhaps the deadliest error of all. By the time the line was revealed, the chaos was already in motion. The delay created a dangerous vacuum of authority where hearsay fueled panic, leading to massacres across the undefined borderlands. In some villages, flags were raised and then lowered as police forces realized they were in the wrong country. Millions found themselves instantly marooned on the "wrong" side of a line they hadn't known existed until it was too late.

This border did not just define territory; it severed ancient water systems, cut through marketplaces, and divided families. It remains a haunting example of how a line drawn in haste on a paper map can permanently scar the geography and soul of a civilization.

Pause for a Moment's Reflection

Chapter 13

Partition: An Unrecognized Tragedy?

The end of British India, which created the separate nations of India and Pakistan, was not merely a political event—it was a humanitarian disaster. The price of freedom and national identity was paid in blood, trauma, and dislocation. Considered one of the bloodiest and largest migrations in history, this great rupture forced millions of people to move, and perhaps more than 2 million people died in the resulting violence. The regions of Kashmir and Punjab were especially affected, and the events of '47 continue to cause tension between the two countries today.

In Punjab and Bengal, the epicenters of the division, butchery engulfed towns and villages. Trains packed with fleeing refugees often arrived at their destinations with no survivors, their passengers brutally slaughtered en route. Entire communities vanished overnight. The border regions, especially in Punjab, witnessed unthinkable horrors that left lasting scars on the survivors and reshaped entire generations.

Among the most haunting crimes was the widespread abduction and sexual violence against women. It is estimated that over 75,000 women were abducted and raped, sometimes by members of other communities—and, tragically, at times by their own. The violence transcended religious lines, revealing the depth of human cruelty unleashed during the chaos. Women's bodies became battlegrounds upon which the honor of entire communities was fought and destroyed.

Religious suppression also took place, especially cruel in areas like Rawalpindi, where entire neighborhoods were razed, and non-Muslims were compelled to convert or flee under the threat of death. These acts, while framed as collective revenge, were deeply twisted with larger processes of ethnic cleansing.

The departure itself was marked by desperate, unplanned movement. Families had only hours to pack their lives into bundles and leave homes that had sheltered generations. Monsoon rains flooded the already limited internal networks, further compounding the misery. With crops destroyed and food in short supply, famine threatened the displaced. Disease and starvation claimed the lives of countless refugees as they journeyed on foot, by bull cart, or in overloaded trains.

After the Second World War, Britain simply no longer had the resources with which to control its greatest imperial asset, and its exit from India was messy and awkwardly improvised. From the viewpoint of the retreating colonizers, however, it was in one way fairly successful. Whereas British rule in India had long been marked by violent revolts and brutal suppressions, the British Army was able to march out of the country with barely a shot fired and only seven casualties. Equally unexpected was the intensity of the ensuing blood-bath.

This tragedy continues to haunt us. The comparison with the death camps is not so far-fetched as it may seem. Partition is central to modern identity in the Indian subcontinent, branded painfully onto the regional consciousness by memories of almost unthinkable violence.

The trauma of this great rupture remained unspoken in many households for decades, passed down through silence and unhealed wounds. Not a single leader ever offered a true apology to those who were displaced. Millions of people died without a final goodbye to their families, without the dignity of a proper funeral. India has yet to build a national memorial honoring those who perished. This silence, this lack of ac-knowledgment, prevents healing.

The 1947 divide was less about putting new boundaries on a map and more about tearing neighbors from shared villages and turning homelands into battlegrounds. Its legacies contin-ue to haunt South Asia, reminding us of both the fragility of peace and the enduring need for compassion and historical review.

Pause for a Moment's Reflection

Chapter 14

Was The 1947 Genocide a Forgotten Chapter in India's History Books?

The violence of 1947, which tore through Punjab, is a dark chapter that remains absent from India's history books. Punjab, a state that once stood strong and tall, now feels powerless—its people burdened by generational trauma and the deep scars left by those tragic events.

Intergenerational trauma, also known as generational or ancestral trauma, is the pain and suffering passed down through generations, often without acknowledgment or healing. This continues to affect the offspring of those who lived through the division of the land, leaving them feeling powerless and disconnected from their past. When we search for records of global genocides, the horrors of 1947 in Punjab are especially absent. The Punjab Partition Genocide is a story untold, a history unrecognized in the very land where it occurred.

Under the 1948 UN Convention, genocide is defined as acts committed with the intent to destroy, in whole or in part, a national, ethnic, racial, or religious group. It is a bitter irony that this definition was codified a mere year after the disastrous events in Punjab—a tragedy that fit every criteria of the convention yet occurred before the world had the legal language to name it.

The brutality surrounding the 1947 border creation included systematic massacres, targeted sexual violence, and forced religious conversions aimed at erasing specific communities from defined territories. The scale and calculated nature of these atrocities against Sikhs, Hindus, and Muslims qualify the campaign of extermination in Punjab as a devastating act of genocide, demanding international recognition and historical inclusion.

To restore the strength and dignity of Punjab, we must move beyond just remembering: we need real action. It is vital to set up a Truth and Justice Commission for the region and country, modeled on global examples, to record testimonies and investigate failures. As survivors pass away, we must quickly recognize their deep pain and honor their immense sacrifices with official memorials.

We must allow survivors and their families to visit the homes of their ancestors, to reconnect with their roots and heal from the wounds of the past. It is time to end the campaign of hate against Pakistan and instead focus on resolving conflicts through dialogue and understanding—something that India has yet to fully achieve. Instead, the policy of the Indian government was to view even its own migrating citizens as security risks & refused to allow them safe passage to visit their own ancestral homes.

That tragedy remains a haunting disappointment, that these people died without any closure, waiting until their deaths for the precious few issued visas to clear, with many still waiting to this day. Millions of Sikhs have visited Pakistan's remaining *gurdwaras* with many openly being embraced with respect & hospitality. They come back with beautiful memories knowing that they are welcomed, with their religion respected. Many *gurdwaras* have been restored & kept open for pilgrims with no discrimination reported by the visiting Sikhs. It's a shame that neighbors refused to resolve their conflict & create a two-way street for citizens to visit & bring harmony to each other.

Punjab, once a thriving region, has gone backwards due to a lack of support and proper systems. But every problem has a solution. We must never minimize the suffering of others: Punjab's people have made the greatest sacrifices—losing everything they owned, from their homes and possessions to their livestock and livelihoods.

It is crucial that the people of India, especially those outside of Delhi, understand the true history of Partition in all its painful detail. We must change the textbooks and build museums dedicated to the event's history in every state, especially in Gujarat, Uttar Pradesh, Bihar, Madhya Pradesh, Odisha, Andhra Pradesh, Karnataka, Tamil Nadu, and Kerala. These states must come to terms with the fact that they too are part of a nation that bears the weight of this forgotten genocide. Only then can we begin to heal the wounds of the past and restore power and pride to Punjab.

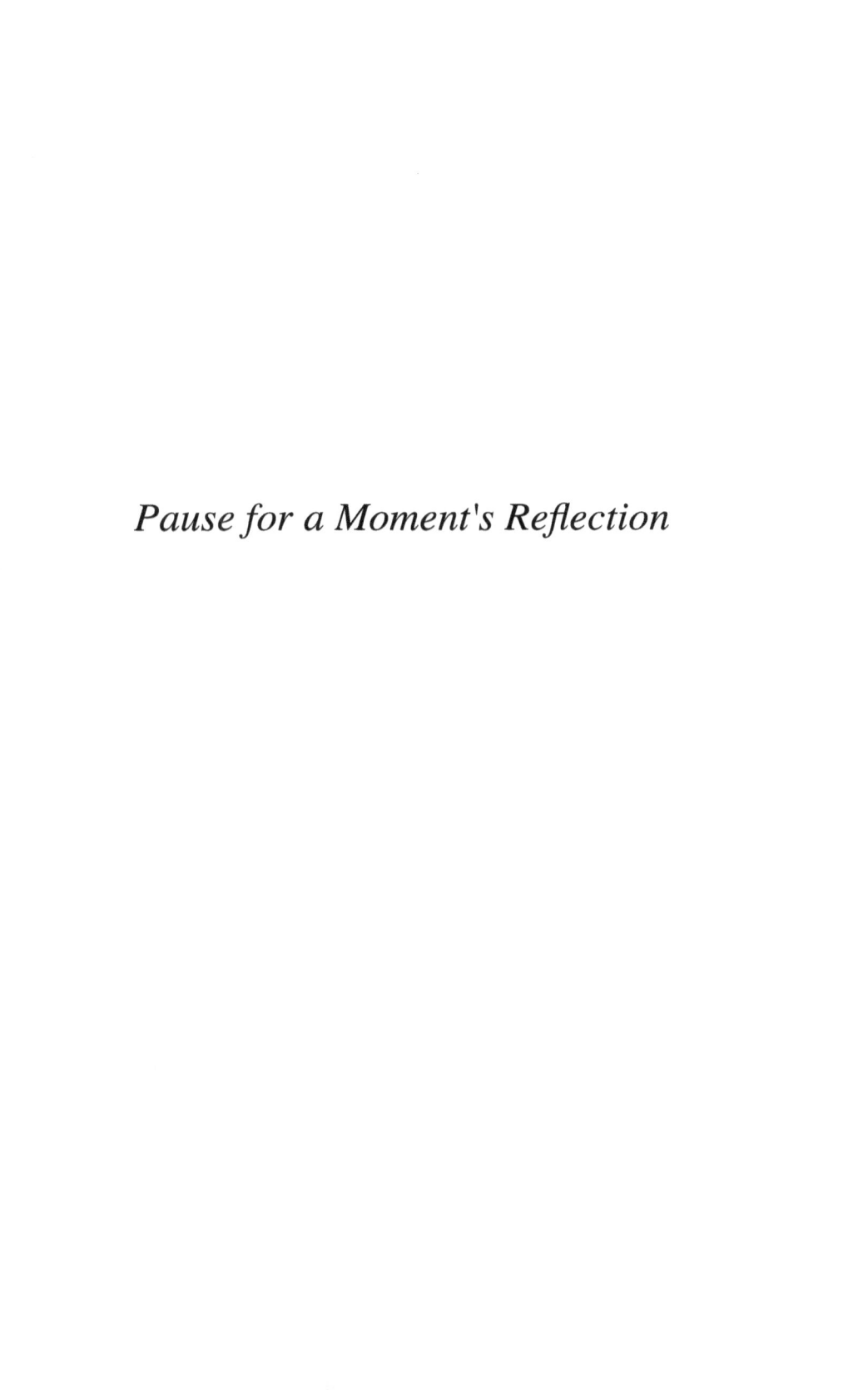

Pause for a Moment's Reflection

Chapter 15

Were Those Affected by Partition Able to Compete with the Rest of India?

When we say "We were unable to compete with the rest of India that didn't experience Partition," we are not just describing an economic lag or a broken culture. We are acknowledging a passed-on imbalance — a break that runs through generations who began life not on equal ground but in the rubble of displacement. This rupture did not simply redraw borders; it redrew the very conditions of opportunity.

Punjab, Bengal, Sindh, the areas most affected by the division of the land — became sites of chaos and reconstruction. Families who once owned land, businesses, or artistic legacies were forced to rebuild from nothing, often in new environments where their past was both irrelevant and burdensome. The rest of India, untouched by this trauma, moved ahead — its institutions intact, its social fabric largely preserved. For the displaced, the struggle was not just for survival, it was for recognition within a system that no longer saw them as equal participants in the nation's progress.

This imbalance cannot be measured just in economic terms. It extended into education, social mobility, and artistic expression. Generations of refugees grew up with broken identities — too burdened by the need to rebuild to invest in higher learning, innovation, or the cultivation of the arts. Their children received their parents enduring spirit, yes, but also a collective fatigue that quieted creative ambitions. The rest of India, meanwhile, carried on with things staying the same: its power structures, institutions, and communities intact. The inequality became invisible and normal.

Artists emerging from families affected by the turmoil of Independence often carried this silence in their work, even unconsciously. Their canvases and compositions reflected the tension between belonging and exclusion — a haunting awareness that their story was secondary to the leading narrative of India's "progress." In contrast, artists from unaffected regions often enjoyed institutional backing, critical recognition, and a lineage of stability that nurtured experimentation.

To say we were unable to compete is not an admission of inferiority but an accusation of the unequal starting lines history imposed. Displacement stripped communities of cultural stability — the thread that allows knowledge, art, and confidence to pass unbroken through time. While others could build upon ancestral structures, we were forced to first build new foundations where none remained. The price of survival was the delay of growth.

Even today, this historical imbalance lingers beneath the surface of India's modern identity. It shapes who gets to define "Indian art," whose stories are archived, and whose voices are dismissed as too regional or political. To confront this truth is to confront the myth of uniform progress — and to recognize that healing requires not only remembering the violence of division but also addressing the quieter, slower violences that followed.

The rest of India moved forward. We, who hold the memory of 1947's divide, built again.

Pause for a Moment's Reflection

Chapter 16

How Did Leadership, Addiction, and Agriculture Fail Punjab?

Punjab, the vibrant Land of Five Rivers, has faced the majority of the trauma of Partition's aftermath more than most regions. While it was once the cradle of India's agricultural prosperity and spiritual strength, the state now deals with political disorder, a devastating drug epidemic, and a crisis in the farming sector. These interwoven challenges have transformed Punjab's socio-economic landscape in deeply troubling ways.

At the heart of Punjab's struggles lies a history of broken political leadership. Widespread corruption and mismanagement have undermined the state's ability to function effectively. This political turmoil worsened radically after Punjab was have undermined the state's ability to function effectively. This political turmoil worsened drastically after Punjab was reorganized in 1966. The redrawing of state boundaries split the province further, forcing rival political groups to constantly form weak alliances and unstable governments. This environment of fragile power-sharing meant that leaders focused only on short-term wins and political survival instead of creating stable, long-term plans for the state's future. Leadership in Punjab frequently changes hands, but the lack of a coherent, long-term vision has left critical issues unresolved. Internal networks, public services, and state resources suffer under these issues, washing away public trust.

One of the most urgent crises facing Punjab is the alarming spread of drug addiction, especially among its youth. Heroin and man-made narcotics have deeply affected communities, tearing through families and futures alike. What was once a land known for vitality and resilience is now battling rising mental health disorders, increased crime rates, and a generation losing its sense of purpose. The impact on Punjab's youth is devastating: school dropout rates have surged, and the horizon of opportunity appears to shrink each year. Economically, the burden is great—healthcare costs rise, productivity falls, and law enforcement resources are stretched thin or open to corruption. The social cost, though harder to measure, is heartbreakingly tangible in the sorrow and dysfunction echoing across families and villages.

Punjab's identity as India's agricultural heartland is also at risk. Farmers face mounting debt, unstable crop prices, and the effects of climate change. Many have been pushed to despair and, tragically, to suicide. Over decades, intensive farming—initially celebrated during the Green Revolution—has negatively affected soil health and depleted groundwater. Sustainable practices have not kept pace with usage, and governmental support has failed to adapt. Inconsistent policies, poor carrying out of relief schemes, and limited access to modern technologies have left farmers with few lifelines.

The consequences of these issues are alarming. Punjab's overall quality of life has gone down. With rising poverty, increased crime, and lacking public services, the social fabric of the state is tearing at the seams. Migration, once a symbol of ambition, now reflects desperation. Many skilled and educated Punjabis leave their homeland in search of better opportunities abroad, further draining the state of human capital. For the less educated, literacy remains an enduring issue, with fluency in both English & Punjabi sorely lacking.

The crisis in Punjab is a complex intersection of political failure, economic despair, and social trauma that demands immediate and unified intervention. To stop this cycle of decline and reclaim the state's rightful place, the once-proud Land of Five Rivers must move beyond analyzing the problems and commit to a single, structured strategy for recovery.

Pause for a Moment's Reflection

Chapter 17

Is There a Comprehensive Plan for Punjab's Recovery and Development?

Punjab continues to carry the heavy burden of The Great Rupture, and its trauma still influences the lives of its people and the region's progress. The first step toward healing is to openly acknowledge this pain and develop a holistic recovery plan centered on unity, transparency, and rebuilding trust.

The people of Punjab have lost faith in their leaders and political systems. Restoring this trust requires transparent governance that operates without hidden agendas. This includes implementing robust, digital anti-corruption measures and establishing independent oversight bodies with real enforcement power. Alongside this, we must foster a culture of public engagement where citizens actively participate in decision-making and feel their voices are genuinely heard and respected. Leadership must emphasize integrity, accountability, and service to nurture trustworthy and effective leaders for the future, moving beyond the identity politics of the past.

Overcoming Punjab's challenges demands a united effort. Community-building programs should encourage solidarity across diverse social segments by focusing on shared goals and mutual respect. Grassroots forums must now prioritize practical problem-solving, creating a generation capable of governing with competence, clarity, and truly effective action.

Mental and emotional healing is equally vital. Strengthening public health and support systems will be necessary to address trauma and the substance abuse crisis, focusing on overall community well-being.

Education plays a pivotal role in empowering Punjab's population. Introducing programs that cultivate critical thinking, decision-making, and personal as well as professional boundary-setting will help shape capable individuals. Training in political strategy, diplomacy, and world history will create informed and strategic thinkers. Comprehensive education in Sikh history will instill pride and a strong sense of identity among the youth.

Reviving Punjab's economic landscape requires thoughtful action and diversification. Economic policies should promote sustainable growth and attract investment in sectors outside traditional agriculture, such as developing food processing units linked to local farms and establishing IT and high-tech hubs in cities to stem the brain drain. Political discourse must mature, focusing on long-term strategy rather than short-term gains. Setting clear boundaries in political practice will help prevent exploitation and corruption. Enhancing physical and spiritual well-being is crucial, promoting physical fitness alongside creating spaces for spiritual healing to reconnect people to their cultural roots. Establishing libraries and community learning centers can foster a culture of reading and lifelong learning.

To begin, forming a dedicated task force of experts in mental health, education, economics, and political science will guide the implementation of the plan. Starting with pilot projects in select areas will allow testing and refinement of programs before application. Continuing tracking and evaluation will ensure that progress is on track and adjustments are made as needed.

Punjab has the potential to transform rapidly with the right approach. By emphasizing unity, clarity, education, and healing, the state can emerge stronger politically, socially, and economically. This vision requires collective effort, mature leadership, and a steadfast commitment to long-term development. Together, Punjab can reclaim its rightful place as a land of prosperity, wisdom, and resilience.

Pause for a Moment's Reflection

Chapter 18

The Success of Gujarat: A Model for Punjab's Transformation?

Gujarat has risen to become one of India's most powerful and successful states, a feat attributed to a combination of guiding long-term decisions, a disciplined society, and sound economic policies. The state's remarkable progress offers valuable lessons for Punjab, which holds great potential for similar growth and prosperity.

One of the key drivers of Gujarat's success is its pro-business environment. The government has routinely encouraged policies that attract both domestic and international investment. By simplifying regulations, improving internal networks, and ensuring ease of doing business, Gujarat has established itself as a thriving hub for industries such as manufacturing and pharmaceuticals.

Strong political leadership has also played a crucial role. Gujarat's leaders have encouraged economic growth through long-term planning and continuing reforms, which have brought industry and job creation. This stable vision contrasts with short-term, incomplete approaches seen elsewhere.

Social discipline and stability have further helped Gujarat's development. The state's ban on alcohol has contributed to lower crime rates, improved public health, and a more productive workforce. This policy has fostered a stable environment that supports sustained economic growth.

Investment in education and skill development completes the picture. Gujarat has focused on giving its population relevant skills that meet industry demands. This ensures that the workforce remains competitive and that opportunities for advancement are available to its citizens.

Given these successes, the question arises: can the Gujarat model be replicated in Punjab? The answer lies in adopting key elements tailored to Punjab's unique context.

A ban on alcohol could bring significant social benefits to Punjab by reducing crime and health problems linked to alcohol abuse. While not a standalone solution, such a ban could be a cornerstone of social reform efforts aimed at improving discipline and focus within the society.

Economically, Punjab can follow Gujarat by introducing business-friendly policies that attract investment and foster entrepreneurship. Streamlining regulations and developing inner networks such as roads and industrial zones will make Punjab a more attractive destination for industries, thereby generating employment and boosting the economy.

Education and skill development must also be prioritized. Punjab should invest in job-based training, critical thinking, and programs for entrepreneurs to prepare its youth for economic opportunities. Partnerships between educational institutions and businesses can make work-based-learning and hands-on learning easier, ensuring a skilled and adaptable workforce.

At the heart of any transformation lies strong political will and leadership. Punjab's leaders must focus on long-term development, combating corruption, ensuring openness, and actively engaging with citizens to build trust and support for reforms.

Social stability, as seen in Gujarat, can be done through public health and community programs. Addressing pressing issues such as drug and alcohol abuse by rehab and awareness campaigns will be crucial to fostering a healthier and more productive population.

Gujarat's journey stands as a statement to the power of forward-thinking leadership, social discipline, and focused economic development. By adopting these lessons, Punjab can overcome its challenges and chart a course toward restored economic success. With a balanced, holistic strategy that integrates social reform, education, economic growth, and transparent policy, Punjab can rise above current struggles and forge a new identity defined by opportunity and strength.

Pause for a Moment's Reflection

Chapter 19

The Sindh Province: How Did a Stateless People Become a Global Success?

The regions most directly impacted by the redrawing of the map — Punjab, Bengal, Sindh — all faced chaos, but the people of Sindh carried a unique weight: the loss of their entire homeland, which became part of a new nation. Sindh was a land of ancient civilization, a place where rivers met the sea, where commerce and culture thrived for centuries. When the borders were drawn, the vast majority of its Hindu and Sikh populations were forced out, leaving behind a richly mixed heritage and powerful commercial networks.

Yes, the massive displacement of the Sindhi community stripped them of their ancestral identity, and it also gave them a new kind of strength. Unlike refugees in some other regions who were settled in concentrated villages, the Sindhi migrants were often scattered across India, from Mumbai and Gujarat to Delhi and beyond. This scattering, while challenging, became their unexpected advantage. It forced them to rely on their tight-knit community bonds and, most importantly, their inner entrepreneurial spirit.

The Sindhi people—who were largely merchants, traders, and businessmen before the split—did not wait for government aid or official programs. They immediately activated their global and pan-Indian trading networks. They carried little physical wealth but brought an invaluable asset: business expertise and a global outlook. This deep-seated culture of commerce became the foundation for their phenomenal recovery.

They established themselves in new cities, often starting from the very bottom with small street stalls or selling goods. They built new towns like Adipur, transforming barren land into thriving commercial hubs. Their success was not granted; it was earned through endless work and financial discipline. This generation of refugees understood that to survive, they had to be self-reliant and masters of their own destiny.

The result is a powerful truth: Sindhi immigrants, both within India and abroad, have become one of the most economically successful and well-integrated communities. They proved that while a homeland can be lost, the spirit of enterprise cannot be taken. Their story is a powerful statement to survival, demonstrating that the trauma of displacement, while painful, did not put out their ability to prosper. They did not just settle; they thrived, contributing greatly to India's economic fabric and achieving recognition globally.

However, even this celebrated success story has a shadow of loss. Yes, they gained wealth and power, but they lost the soil, the language, and the ancient temples of their ancestors. Their success is a powerful story against being left behind to start all over, but it does not erase the historical injustice of being cut from their roots.

We must recognize their triumph not as a simple happy ending, but as the hard-won achievement of a stateless people who refused to be defeated by history. The Sindhi story is an important lesson: that true success is measured not just by how much is rebuilt, but by the unbreakable will to keep the flame of one's identity burning, even in a foreign land.

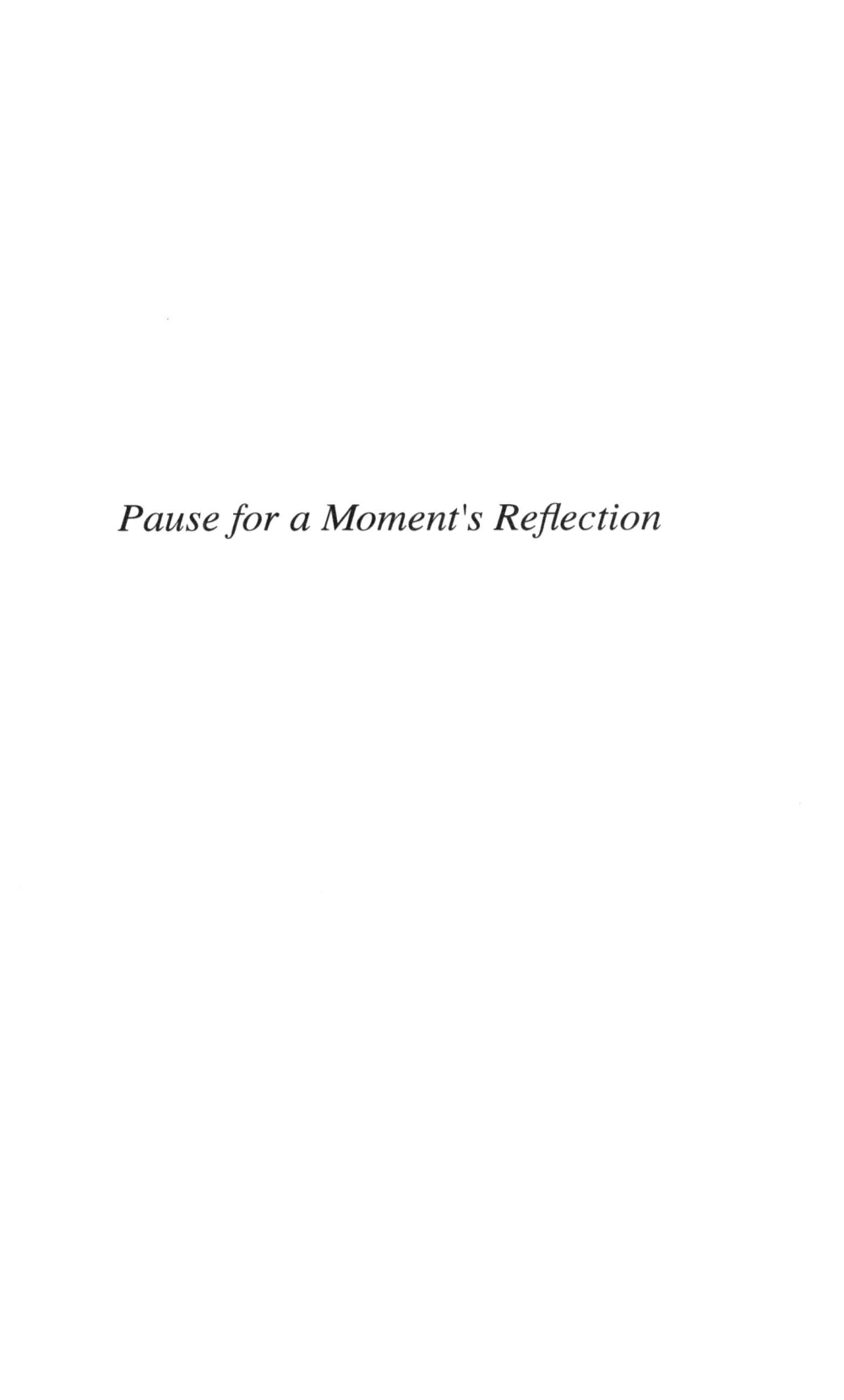

Pause for a Moment's Reflection

Chapter 20

Can Sindhi Triumph Be Turned into Punjabi Action?

T he Sindhi story offers a powerful and painful contrast to the struggles detailed in the chapters focused on Punjab. The achievement of the Sindhi people, built strongly on business spirit and self-reliance, offers a direct and hard-won lesson for Punjab's economic revival. They proved that business networks, not dependence on state handouts, are the true currency of survival.

Punjab must adopt this aggressive spirit of internal entrepreneurial growth. We must shift our focus from waiting for outside investment to cultivating our own local businesses and taking advantage of our global Punjabi diaspora as a powerful economic force. As noted in the recovery plan, good economic policies must focus on sustainable growth and local support. The Sindhi community achieved this through need; Punjab must achieve it through taking note and then action.

However, the Sindhi narrative also holds a warning that we must follow: achievement gained by suppressing trauma or cultural memory is an incomplete victory. For generations, the cultural identity of many Sindhis was allowed to fade for the sake of their success in new lands, the price paid for their achievement. Punjab cannot afford this hidden, internal loss.

To truly honor our past and secure our future, Punjab must couple the push for economic revival with the essential components of social and emotional healing. We must act with clarity and urgency to:

1. Create "Fast-Track" Vocational Skill Centers: Specialized training centers focused on high-demand global trade skills (social media, finance, digital commerce) to rapidly teach the population marketing, a modern twist on the Sindhi community's post-Partition focus on business skills.

2. Create a Diaspora Mentorship Program: A trusted, high-accountability program connecting successful Punjabi and Sindhi entrepreneurs abroad directly with small businesses and startups in Punjab, providing expertise and direct network access rather than just financial donations.

3. Develop a State-Level Anti-Corruption & Accountability: An independent body with public representation and direct official powers to immediately address political corruption and make sure all new economic and social programs are

managed with the total openness demanded by a population that has lost almost all trust.

In addition, based on the Sindhi model of self-reliance and use of global networking, Punjab must also launch these new programs:

- Establish a Global Punjabi Business Network (GPBN): A formal, government-supported body dedicated not to receiving aid, but fostering investment, mentorship, and immediate trading opportunities between Punjabi entrepreneurs in India and the diaspora worldwide. This follows in the footsteps of the Sindhi community's pre-existing commercial ties.

- Create Localized "Seed Capital" Funds: Community-managed micro-loan and seed investment funds, especially to support the immediate creation of small-scale businesses by youth and women in local towns, mirroring the quick activation of capital seen after Sindhi resettling.

- Launch a Cultural & Oral History Project: An urgent, state-sponsored plan to record and archive the memories, songs, and language of living 1947 survivors across Punjab. This combats the cultural silence that followed the Sindhi displacement, making sure that cultural identity is preserved while economic rebuilding occurs.

The journey of the Sindhi people shows that unity is a powerful force. But for Punjab, true recovery and dignity needs more than just rebuilding; they demand we rebuild *better*, with both economic vision and moral clarity. This demands a unified drive to transform Punjab's narrative into a legacy of thriving, independent strength.

Pause for a Moment's Reflection

Chapter 21

Healing the Wounds of Partition —
Is There a Path Forward?

Healing from the trauma of the Great Rupture is a long and complex journey, one that extends its impact from individuals to families, communities, and nations. For survivors and their offspring, the process of healing must address the psychological, social, cultural, and historical dimensions of this profound and devastating split.

Public acknowledgment is the first crucial step toward healing. Governments, institutions, and communities must recognize the pain endured by survivors of the Great Rupture. This can be achieved through local memorial events and community forums that validate survivors' experiences, creating vital spaces for shared historical memory where private grief finds a public voice.

Mental health support is also vital. Establishing trauma-informed counseling services, support centers, and helplines can provide survivors and their families with professional care. Support groups offer survivors a space to connect, share, and process their experiences together. Therapies that understand intergenerational trauma can help younger generations make sense of inherited pain.

Community engagement offers another venue for connection and support. Local leaders, both religious and civic, can play a powerful role in promoting healing and offering safe spaces for dialogue. Community centers and interfaith programs can rebuild the social fabric torn by the division of the nation.

Education plays an essential role in healing. Including the history and human impact of Partition in schools promotes awareness and empathy in younger generations. Public awareness campaigns further support this mission, challenging lingering issues and stereotypes while fostering compassion.

Economic and social support remain necessary for many survivors and their families. Providing financial aid, job training, and employment programs can help overcome long-standing hardship. Scholarships for the offspring of survivors can break cycles of poverty and empower future generations.

Holistic health and wellness programs, which include physical health services and wellness techniques like nutrition, movement, and meditation, also contribute to healing. These practices support survivors' overall well-being and help manage the stress and trauma of the past.

The preservation of memory is a powerful tool for healing. Documenting and sharing personal stories not only honors survivors but also educates others and preserves history for the future. Supporting research into the events of 1947's long-term effects can help develop better policies and therapeutic practices.

Legal and policy frameworks are essential to secure justice and provide tangible support. Governments can provide payments for survivors, provide legal aid to resolve property and citizenship issues, and create systems that uphold the dignity of survivors.

Resolution must be both local and cross-border. Interfaith dialogue and cooperative peace plans between India and Pakistan can help address historical feelings of being wronged and promote mutual understanding. These efforts aim to foster peace through truth, compassion, and collaboration.

Finally, long-term monitoring and evaluation are necessary to ensure that support programs remain effective. Oversight bodies should regularly assess survivors' needs and adjust resources accordingly, maintaining a commitment to sustained healing.

Art and culture have always been powerful forms of creating legacy. Funding cultural projects and encouraging artistic expression offer survivors and their families creative ways to process trauma and preserve identity. Whether through poetry, painting, music, or film, these acts of memory can serve as both personal healing and collective testimony.

Together, these approaches form a wholesale and compassionate roadmap for healing. While the scars from the creation of India and Pakistan may never fully fade, meaningful support, acknowledgment, and community can bring light to the darkness, offering survivors and their children the hope and dignity they deserve.

Pause for a Moment's Reflection

Chapter 22

What are the First Steps to Start Peace Talks?

Starting peace talks between two conflicting parties, such as India and Pakistan, requires careful planning and a well-structured approach to foster constructive dialogue and work towards a lasting resolution. The process begins with comprehensive initial measures. This includes in-depth assessments to understand the current state of relations, identify key issues, and appreciate the interests and concerns of both sides. Such groundwork is essential for setting a realistic and focused agenda for the negotiations.

Building internal consensus is equally important. Both governments and all relevant stakeholders—military, political, and civil society alike—must be committed to the peace process. Without wide-ranging support, any dialogue is at risk. Often, neutral third parties or international organizations are brought in for mediation. Their impartial role is to guide discussions, offer expert advice, and help manage the process to ensure fairness and effectiveness.

Establishing reliable communication channels is the next vital step. Direct lines of dialogue between leaders allow for formal engagement through meetings or diplomatic exchanges. In addition, backchannel diplomacy—private, informal communications—can be instrumental in building trust and resolving sensitive preliminary matters, setting the stage for official talks.

Once dialogue is established, the parties must clearly define the objectives and scope of the peace talks. This involves outlining specific issues to be addressed, such as territorial disputes, security concerns, or economic cooperation, and agreeing on the structure and timeline for discussions. However the talks are structured, clarity helps prevent misunderstandings.

Preparing a detailed agenda follows. This agenda should prioritize the core concerns of both sides, ensuring a balanced approach that addresses protests without sidelining key topics. Terms of reference are drafted to set guidelines for conduct, privacy, and the roles and responsibilities of all participants, providing a framework within which the talks will proceed.

Formal peace talks are then started through scheduled meetings in neutral, supporting environments. Skilled moderators often play a critical role in guiding discussions and maintaining focus on constructive outcomes.

Restoring trust between parties is a conscious process. Confidence-building measures such as ceasefires, humanitarian exchanges, or cooperative plans in less divisive areas can foster trust. Clarity throughout the negotiations, along with regular communication to the public and stakeholders, helps manage expectations and build wider support for the peace process.

Addressing the core issues requires detailed negotiation. Both parties must be prepared to make compromises and seek solutions acceptable to all. As agreements take shape, formal documents are drafted outlining resolutions to ensure commitments are upheld.

Securing endorsements is critical for credibility. This includes gaining the backing of governments, political leaders, and relevant institutions. Approval by governing bodies formalizes and confirms the agreements.

Monitoring the agreed terms require the creating of oversight bodies—joint committees or international observers—to track progress and ensure accountability. Regular reviews allow for adjustments to address emerging challenges or concerns.

Finally, peace talks should promote peace beyond political agreements. Cultural exchanges, collaborative projects, and public education play an essential role in healing historical wounds and building sustainable peace. Long-term peace-building efforts must be supported through investments in economic development, education, and community engagement.

In conclusion, starting peace talks demands careful planning, steady commitment, and cooperation from all involved parties. By following these steps, leaders can create a helpful environment for dialogue, confront pressing issues, and pave the way toward a lasting and peaceful resolution.

*   *   *

A Final Word -The Moral Imperative of Peace

Beyond the technical steps and diplomatic protocols, there is a moral imperative that must guide the peace process. A foundational "rule of thumb" in human relations is the necessity of honoring one's neighbors, understanding that "love your neighbor" is a condition for integrity and harmony. Conflict between neighbors often reflects a failure to look inward rather than an issue with the other side. The policy of 'divide and rule' is not a sustainable foundation for neighboring nations or human communities. The tragic reality is that the people who were divided once shared ancestral land and lived peacefully; they were not born enemies. It is often the cynical actions of politicians that create these divisions, leading to brutality and the taking of land from what were once peaceful neighbors. India has historically been a land of many cultures and religions, a place that, despite countless invasions, always stayed unified in its core culture; The Great Rupture shattered that unity, permanently altering South Asia's identity. Sustainable peace, therefore, demands an end to political manipulation and a return to the basic wisdom of coexistence.

Pause for a Moment's Reflection

Chapter 23

Are Sikhs the Ideal Neutral Party for India-Pakistan Peace?

To understand why Sikhs are the ideal party to broker peace between these two countries, we must first explore the conditions that forged the Sikh nation into the fierce & fearless faith they are today. The martial tradition of this community was created over many centuries of fighting to defend themselves against various empires, especially the Mughals. After the repression of their early Gurus, the Sikhs changed their identity, adopting the concept of the Saint-Soldier (*Sant Sipahi*) under the guidance of Guru Hargobind Ji and later, Guru Gobind Singh Ji. This idea created a religious duty to defend justice and truth, making military service and discipline core parts of the Sikh faith. By the early 19th century, this spiritual drive was turned into the powerful state of the

Sikh Empire under Maharaja Ranjit Singh, whose highly trained Khalsa Army controlled a large region and was considered one of the strongest native armies in South Asia.

When the British began their long period of colonial rule, they quickly understood and used this deep-seated fighting tradition. The British, who had fought intensely against the Khalsa Army, officially labeled Sikhs as a "Martial Race," a controversial title that directed the community's fighting spirit into the British Indian Army. Throughout the late 19th and early 20th centuries, this community served widely in British wars all over the world, from the two World Wars to conflicts in Africa and the Middle East, winning a huge number of military awards. This tradition ensured that when the British finally left in 1947, a highly skilled and military-wise community remained in the newly independent country, ready to dedicate its long history of service to protecting the Indian nation.

Since the birth of independent India, the Sikh community has stood as a towering pillar of strength, duty, and patriotic devotion—especially within the ranks of the Indian Armed Forces. Even though Sikhs make up less than 2% of India's population, they have historically contributed between 10–15% of the Indian Armed Forces. This striking figure reflects a dedicated tradition of service, courage, and sacrifice that far outweighs their presence in numbers. The legacy of Sikh bravery did not begin in 1947; that tradition carried seamlessly into independent India, where Sikhs became the backbone of the country's defense during every major military conflict—from the wars against Pakistan in 1947, 1965, and 1971, to the Kargil conflict of 1999, and even during peacekeeping missions abroad.

The Sikh Regiment, one of the most decorated units in the Indian Army, has earned countless honors for its bravery. In the 1965 war with Pakistan, it was the Sikh Regiment that strongly defended the crucial town of Asal Uttar, turning the tide of battle. The battlefield was so deeply marked by Sikh courage that it became known as "Patton Nagar" due to the number of Pakistani Patton tanks destroyed by Indian forces led by Sikh soldiers.

In the 1971 war that led to the creation of Bangladesh, Lieutenant General Jagjit Singh Aurora, himself a Sikh, accepted Pakistan's surrender—the largest surrender since World War II—marking a historic victory for India. It was a moment that revealed the quiet leadership and military brilliance that Sikh officers have frequently brought to the armed forces.

The core concept of the Saint-Soldier demands that martial duty must always go with an unwavering humanitarian commitment. The Sikh Gurus demonstrated this by placing the defense of the weak above all else, often standing up for communities outside of their own faith. This dual commitment to courage *and* compassion provides the perfect template for diplomacy in a conflict zone.

The rule of Maharaja Ranjit Singh is an excellent example of this principle in politics. His Sikh Empire was defined by secular governance, where Hindus, Muslims, and Sikhs were appointed to the highest ranks of his court and army based solely on merit, not religion. His model demonstrates a historical desire and capacity for fostering trust and managing complex ethnic co-existence across the very region that was later violently divided.

Despite this unshakeable dedication to India's defense, the Sikh community holds a unique and critical position that makes it an ideal neutral third party for assisting peace talks between India and Pakistan. This is a community that possesses a profound moral claim on both sides of the border. They were promised a special state by Congress leaders and were later betrayed. They lost their ancestral homes, sacred shrines, and entire economic base in what became Pakistan, yet they remain one of the most patriotic communities in India. This dual history of betrayal and immense sacrifice gives them a moral authority and a perspective of shared loss—they can speak credibly to the pain of both sides.

Furthermore, their commitment to global and national peace, proven through their vital role in disaster relief, rescue missions, and UN peacekeeping missions overseas, combined with their unmatched military bravery, demonstrates the integrity and ability required to bridge the deep gap of mistrust between the two states. The Saint-Soldier ideal translates directly into the diplomatic arena: the courage to stand up for justice, the discipline to negotiate complex issues, and the humanitarian spirit to desire peace for all—*Sarbat da Bhala*.

The Sikh soldier is dedicated to the defense of India's borders, and the Sikh diplomat is uniquely poised to transcend them and heal the division. It is time we look past the headlines of conflict and recognize this community not just as guardians of our nation, but as the only logical bridge-builders of South Asia. By leveraging their history of inclusive governance and their profound commitment to service above self, Sikhs offer both nations a trusted, neutral path forward, one paved by sacrifice and illuminated by the hope of unity.

Despite this commitment to loyalty and sacrifice, for now the story of Sikh contributions to India's defense and diplomacy remains largely untold in textbooks, media, and public discourse. Memorials are few, and mentions are often brief. Yet, every Indian flag that flies freely, every child who sleeps safely, owes something to a Sikh soldier who stood watch under the stars.

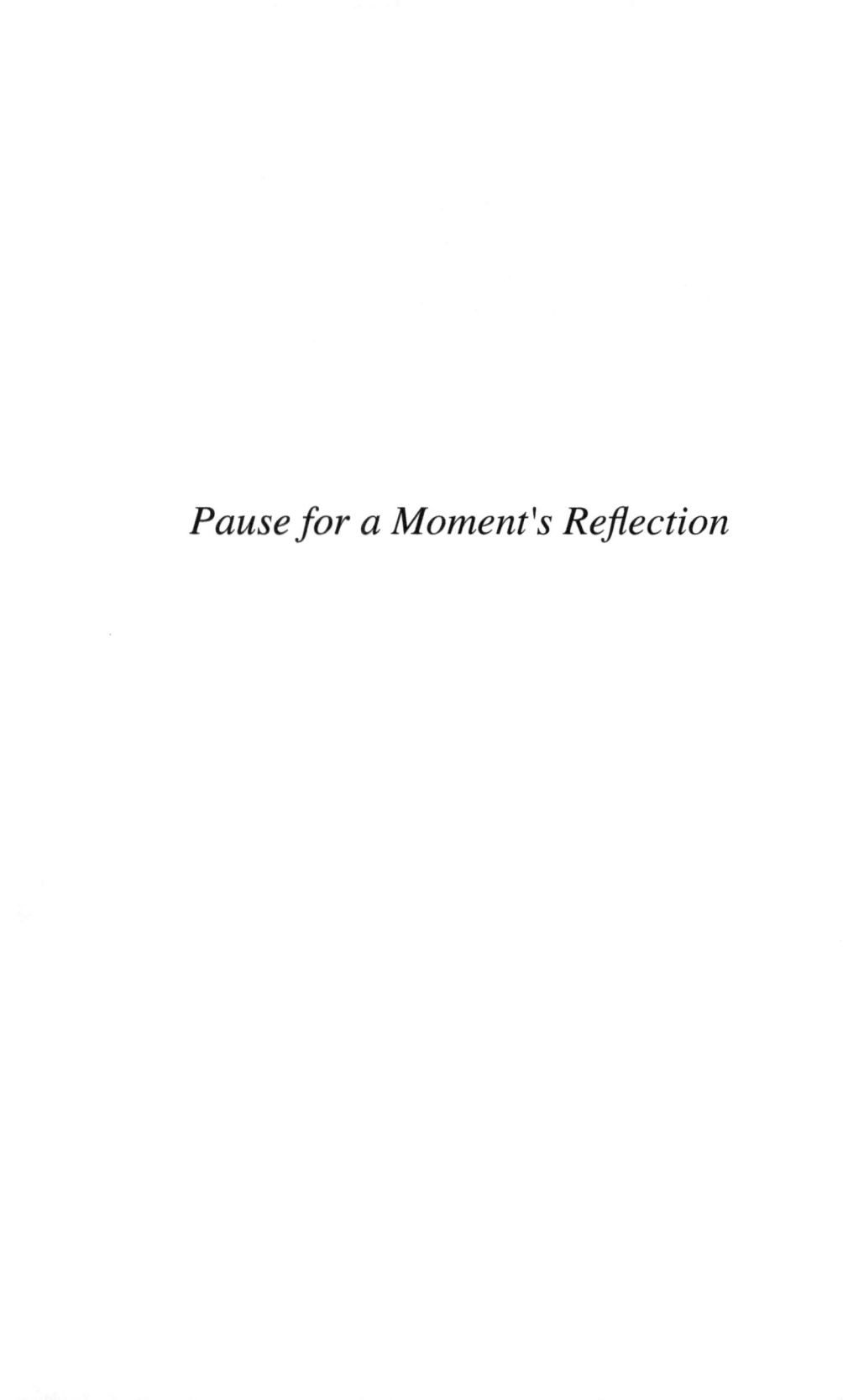

Pause for a Moment's Reflection

Chapter 24

A Peace Treaty Between India and Pakistan?

For generations, the echoes of 1947 have haunted families like mine, shaping our stories through absence and silence. As an artist, I have always felt that our pain still lingers in the spaces between borders — not only on maps, but in memory, identity, and belonging.

A Peace Treaty Between India and Pakistan is my way of re-thinking what healing might look like if art could speak the language of diplomacy. It is a symbolic act — a dialogue written in the language of treaties and guided by mutual compassion, not lust for power. Each article in this treaty is a gesture of hope, an attempt to rewrite a future where understanding replaces suspicion and where peace is not negotiated but created, like a painting, layer by layer.

Through this work, I seek to correct history by confronting it — to offer a space where the human cost of division is acknowledged, and where imagination becomes a tool for peace. If the wounds of 1947 were drawn by political lines, then perhaps empathy and dialogue can begin to erase them.

Preamble

We, the representatives of the Republic of India and the Islamic Republic of Pakistan, in a spirit of cooperation, understanding, and mutual respect, acknowledge the vital importance of achieving lasting peace and stability in South Asia. Recognizing the deep historical bitterness and conflicts that have affected our nations and peoples, we enter into this treaty to foster peaceful coexistence, enhance mutual relations, and promote prosperity for both countries.

Article 1: Ceasefire and Military De-escalation

Both nations hereby agree to an immediate and wholesale ceasefire along all borders, including the Line of Control (LoC) in Jammu and Kashmir. To prevent misunderstandings and accidental confrontations, both parties commit to reducing military deployments and activities in border areas. A joint review process will be set up to monitor and ensure full compliance with these ceasefire measures.

Article 2: Dialogue and Diplomatic Relations

India and Pakistan commit to continuing and constructive mutual dialogue addressing all outstanding issues, including territorial disputes, trade, and security concerns. A framework for regular meetings between government officials will be put into place to support ongoing communication and negotiation. Any disputes shall be resolved peacefully by mediation, with no recourse to violence.

Article 3: Trade and Economic Cooperation

Both nations pledge to expand trade relations by reducing tariffs and non-tariff barriers, encouraging mutual economic cooperation. Joint economic projects, including development programs, will be explored for the benefit of both parties. Cross-border investments will be encouraged to foster economic growth and shared prosperity.

Article 4: People-to-People Relations

To strengthen the bonds between our peoples, cultural, educational, artistic, and sports exchanges will be promoted. Travel and tourism between India and Pakistan will be held through simplified visa procedures. Both nations will collaborate on humanitarian projects addressing common challenges in health, education, and disaster relief.

Article 5: Environmental and Water Resource Management

Recognizing shared environmental responsibilities, India and Pakistan will cooperate on conservation and sustainability plans, including climate change and protection of natural resources. A fair water-sharing framework will be established to manage water resources within boundaries, ensuring sustainability and mutual benefit.

Article 6: Implementation and Monitoring

An Application Committee, made up of officials from both governments, will oversee the enforcement of this treaty. Regular reviews will assess progress and ensure compliance, addressing any emerging issues. Disagreements regarding the treaty's interpretation or application will be resolved through dialogue.

Article 7: Period of Time and Amendments

This treaty shall remain in effect from here on, subject to reviews and updates agreed upon by both parties. Any amendments must be made by mutual consent in writing.

Signatures

In witness of which, the undersigned representatives of the Republic of India and the Islamic Republic of Pakistan have signed this Peace Treaty on [Date], in [City], affirming their commitment to peace and cooperation.

For the Republic of India:

[Name]

[Title]

[Signature]

For the Islamic Republic of Pakistan:

[Name]

[Title]

[Signature]

This treaty provides a foundational framework for peace and cooperation, addressing historical conflicts while paving the way toward a positive and prosperous relationship between India and Pakistan.

Pause for a Moment's Reflection

Chapter 25

My Simple Request to the Leaders

The Partition of India and the succeeding division of Punjab were engineered to solve a political problem, but the real, tragic results were deeply human and moral. The most profound trauma was the immediate and violent collapse of a centuries-old social fabric: a once united population turned against each other overnight, seeing trusted neighbors as strangers and countrymen as bitter enemies preoccupied only with blame and division. This frenzy of communal hatred ensured that the wounds would remain raw for generations.

On a physical and cultural level, the tragedy was absolute. Ancestral homes, vibrant marketplaces, sacred places of worship, and centuries of shared history were brutally destroyed, reused or abandoned, leaving an unfixable cultural and spiritual void.

Crucially, in the wake of this genocide and displacement, the colonial architects of the divide—the British—escaped untouched. They left India having avoided all accountability for the chaos they unleashed, leaving the successor nations burdened with a shared history of trauma, mistrust, and an unfinished judgment. This legacy of division and unaddressed pain demands an urgent response.

My simple request to the leaders of my homeland is this: Lead with integrity, compassion, and a genuine commitment to healing the wounds of the past. Unite the people, rebuild what has been lost, and create a future where every citizen can thrive. Let us restore our land's strength and dignity, and work towards a legacy of peace and prosperity for generations to come. To rebuild a strong nation, we must fully understand the impact of colonial behavior and create a complete, transparent plan to address the aftermath of the genocide that followed the end of British India. This plan must be clear, well-thought-out, and focused on uniting the people of India. Strong, healthy-minded leaders are essential to guiding this process and fostering true unity. The time for healing is now, and it is important that we take action this year: I love the country of my birth and only want the best for all people by speaking truth to its leaders. I am determined to witness Punjab's transformation from the scars of 1947 within my lifetime. The journey toward renewal and strength must begin today.

Pause for a Moment's Reflection

SECTION 2: A HISTORY THROUGH ART

ARTIST STATEMENT

I am Tanya Momi, an artist whose personal journey is deeply woven with themes of strength, survival, and healing. My work—shaped by my experiences as an immigrant and being born to refugee parents—is a powerful, personal statement on finding empowerment within challenge.

When I create my Partition paintings, the process is intensely therapeutic. Tears often stream down my face as I connect with the raw, inherited pain. I feel a profound sense of honor in being able to speak about this art, knowing that no one else can fully express the stories that reside within me.

These paintings are not merely historical records; they are deeply personal vessels of inherited memory. As a first-generation daughter of independent India, I carry the untold truths and the suffering of my refugee grandparents and parents.

This history—marked by the displacement of over 20 million people, the loss of an estimated 2 million lives, and the trauma and horrific crimes committed—is an impact that cannot be overlooked. Through my art, I aim to convey the magnitude of this great tragedy and its lasting effect on homes, livelihoods, and mental health.

I feel a profound duty to honor these struggles and to give voice to the memories of those affected. History has a tendency to repeat itself; therefore, we must never forget the sacrifices made. My ultimate hope is to create awareness, empathy, and a deeper understanding—so that we may learn, heal, and ensure this tragic human experience is acknowledged and honored, preventing the mistakes of the past from being repeated. It is my sincere desire that these paintings will one day travel to museums in both India and Pakistan, bridging the divisions between neighbors and allowing coming generations to understand the history and ancestral stories portrayed in this art.

Thank you for witnessing this journey; I am honored to share these stories with you.

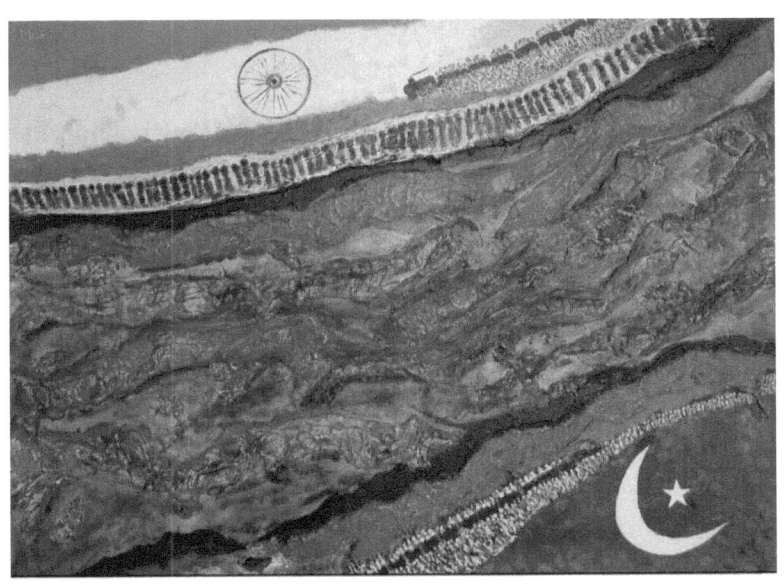

1. Title: *Divided*
Medium: Acrylic & Mixed Media
Size: 30x40
Date: 8.14.2019

Description: Millions of people were uprooted from their homeland, migrating on foot, in bull carts, and by train. The division of the land into two countries affected both sides of my grandparents and my parents. This painting illustrates the tragic story of the creation of India and Pakistan, as told by my mother and father.

The top left-hand side features the tricolor flag, showing the arrival of a train into India. The train was so full that my father's family had to sit on the side of the engine for three days. They thankfully arrived safely, unlike the passengers of many other "ghost trains." The vertical black lines represent the bodies of those slaughtered during the transit, lined up as a haunting memorial. Meanwhile, the brown mud slides symbolize the rainy month of August 1947, when the newly divided rivers overflowed with bodies and blood—symbolized by the parallel gauze on the canvas.

The bottom right side depicts people and trains leaving from India for Pakistan. I incorporated my emotions and feelings, drawn from the stories I heard from both sides of my family. As a first generation born in independent India, I learned of these events when we visited Pakistan in 1971 to see my mother's home in Lahore. My father, who was a 12-year-old forced to flee, described the events shown in this painting: he managed to make the journey to newly-formed India by escaping the mobs and surrounding violence.

As a young girl, I was deeply affected by learning about Partition—the devastation of leaving everything behind, escaping death and disease, and surviving for three years as refugees living in basic camps.

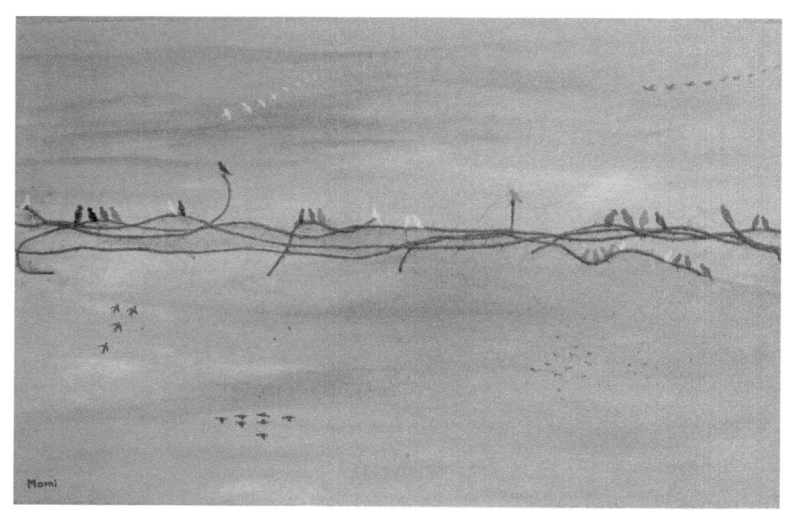

123

2. Title: *Birds Without Borders*
Medium: Acrylic
Size: 16 x 20
Date: 10.16.2019

Description: These vibrant birds, perched delicately on the border, embody the essence of freedom. They soar across the skies without requiring permission, their feathers reflecting the colors of the flags of India and Pakistan. Like peaceful messengers, they travel unseen boundaries, crossing back and forth without harm or hesitation. In their boundless world, divisions do not exist—a powerful reminder of the unity and harmony humanity could achieve if we embraced empathy and compassion. These birds inspire a vision of a world without borders, where freedom and connection thrive beyond barriers.

3. Title: *Clouds Know No Borders*
Medium: Acrylic
Size: 16X20
Date 9.20.2019

Description: Clouds pass the borders and rain without permission. Steam rises from the rivers, going up to the clouds and crossing border lines. The unseen rivers selflessly contribute to the moisture in the air, a five-piece symphony of the sound of rain, thunder, storms, wind, and rushing water. This is the same water that has been here since the Earth came into existence: we are still drinking, bathing, & worshiping this substance that connects us to the birth of our world. The same clouds go back and forth between divided Punjab, offering the same abundance.

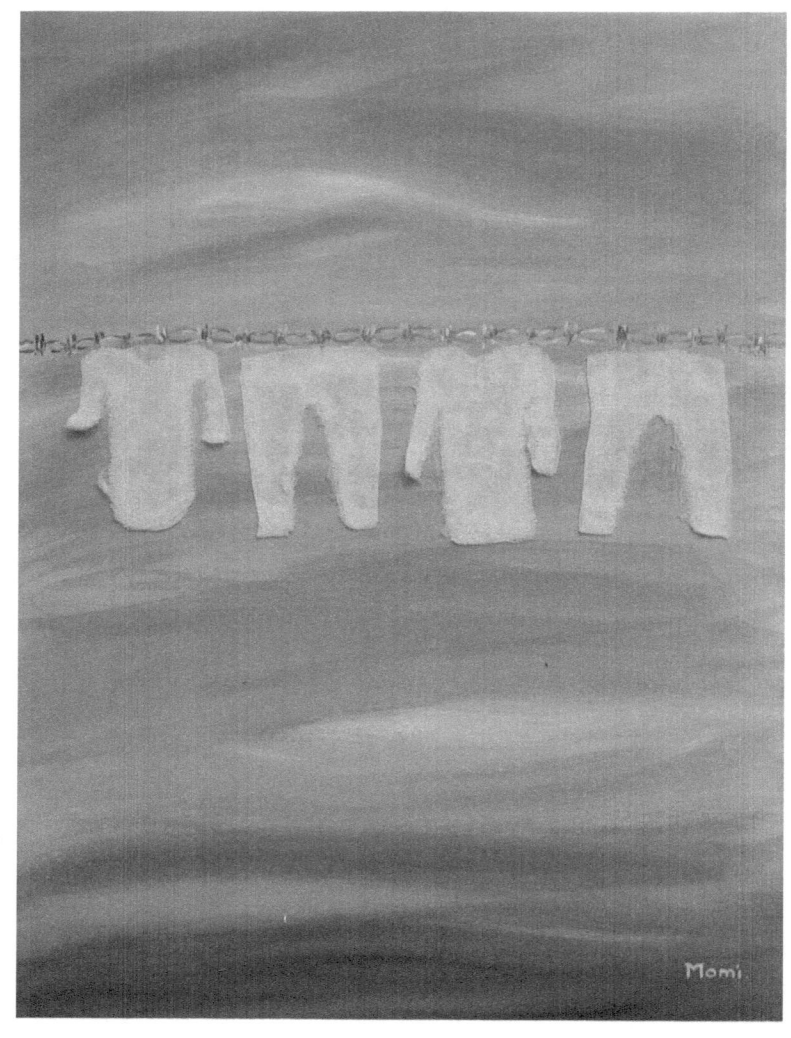

4. Title: *Neighbors Never Met Again*
Medium: Acrylic & Gauze
Size: 18x24
Date: 9.20.2019

Description: In this somber and deeply moving canvas, we find a powerful narrative of separation, division, and the bittersweet memories of unity lost.

With the backdrop of a tight barbed-wire fence, we see a collection of clothes gently hanging on the wire like silent witnesses to a tale of lives intertwined and then torn apart. These clothes, composed of gauze, symbolize a shared existence between neighbors who once hung their laundry on common clotheslines.

The painful emotions coming from this painting are strongly felt. What were once neighboring communities, united in their daily chores and in the simple act of drying clothes, now find themselves separated by the harsh reality of geopolitical boundaries. The Indian Kurta, once paired with the Pakistani Shalwar, and the Pakistani Kameez, once paired by the Indian Pajama, now stand isolated from their natural counterparts.

These clothes, fluttering in the wind, are a statement to a time when neighbors were more than just nearby houses; they represent bonds of friendship and kinship, without concern for borders and political divisions. This artwork creates a sense of longing and wishing for the return of those moments when unity prevailed over division.

"Neighbors Never Met Again" is more than just a painting; it is a powerful and moving reminder of the human cost of separation. It invites us to reflect on the shared histories that often transcend the lines drawn on maps, and to mourn the loss of connections that once were so beautifully interwoven.

May this artwork serve as a tribute to the enduring spirit of unity and as a call to remember that, beyond borders and boundaries, there is always the potential for reconnection among neighbors who once shared clotheslines and so much more.

5. Title: *Lost Without You*
Medium: Acrylic
Size: 16x20
Date: 6.7.2025

Description: In the turbulent and heart-wrenching chapter of the Great Rupture, in the passed down stories of human tragedy and loss, there existed another sorrowful narrative, that of the faithful horses left behind by their owners who said their final goodbyes.

"Lost Without You" captures the essence of this untold tale. In the midst of chaos, as millions of people embarked on terrible journeys, their loyal companions were left behind, standing around confused and abandoned. These beautiful creatures, once the trusted companions of their owners, now found themselves without familiar faces to guide them.

The canvas portrays the haunting loneliness of these horses, their eyes reflecting a sense of loss and uncertainty. They stand in an open landscape, with noble forms a statement to their spirit in the face of abandonment. The question arises, "Who will claim these horses now?" In a world torn apart by division, the fate of these loyal beings hangs in the balance. They are a touching reminder of the indirect victims of human conflicts, the innocent souls who bear the weight of decisions made by others.

"Lost Without You" invites us to think about the untold stories of sacrifice and separation that unfolded during Independence. It urges us to recognize the shared pain of not just humans but all beings who bear witness to the disturbance of history. May this artwork serve as a tribute to the silent sufferers who were the horses left behind and as a reminder of the profound connections between humans and animals. In their eyes, we find a reflection of our desire for reunion and the universal hope that one day, those who are lost will find their way home.

6. Title: *Difficult Times*
Medium: Acrylic and Gauze
Size: 30x40
Date: 9.30.2019

Description: This artwork bears witness to the personal struggles and resilience of one extraordinary woman — my maternal grandmother.

As a young girl, I vividly remember my grandmother's focused determination, sown into my heart like the golden threads she carefully extracted from her beautiful garments. These garments, adorned with lush Indian embroidery, such as Zari Tilla work, Gota work, Tilla Gold threads, and precious pearls, became more than just clothing — they transformed into a lifeline.

The painful memories associated with those threads tell a powerful tale of survival and sacrifice. My grandmother, a strong and enduring woman, sold these treasures to provide for her family. Her husband, my grandfather, had tragically passed away in 1963, leaving behind a widow with two married daughters and the responsibility of caring for three more daughters and a young son. The sole source of income became the modest pension from the police department where my grandfather had dedicated his service.

Their journey had begun earlier, driven by the foresight to leave Lahore, which was dangerously close to the border with India, before the riots and violence after Independence could engulf them. The family had once lived in a grand house, a "Haveli," in Lahore, now but a memory.

My own recollections of my grandmother's house, filled with warmth and love, stand in stark contrast to the hardships she faced. She was born in British India under the British flag, but her memories were carved in Pakistan under the flag of the newly formed nation. In her golden years, she resided in independent India under the tricolor flag.

7. Title: *One Day, We Will Be One Again*
Medium: Acrylic
Size: 16 x 20
Date: 9.9.2019

Description: Inspired by my father, Balbir Singh Momi, who always believed that one day India and Pakistan could reunite as one, this painting captures the spirit of hope, unity, and love. My father often spoke of the harmony that once existed, where people lived side by side with deep understanding and affection.

I vividly recall visiting Lahore with my father to see my mother's childhood home. The warmth of the welcome we received was overwhelming—the entire neighborhood came out to greet us. My mother's childhood friends reunited with her, and as we sat in her old home, tears flowed freely, filled with emotion and longing. The care we experienced was un-matched, a statement to the deep bonds that cross borders.

This painting merges the flags of India and Pakistan, symbol-izing the dream of unity and the shared heritage of both na-tions. It serves as a reminder that—despite the pain of separa-tion—art, music, food, and stories have the power to bring people together. While the dream of unity may seem far away, through imagination, compassion, and hope, we can envision a future of peace and togetherness.

8. Title: *Kashmir vs Kashmir*
Medium: Acrylic and Gauze
Size: 16x20
Date: 3.22.2020

Description: In the chilling narrative painted on this canvas, "Kashmir vs Kashmir," the reality of human suffering and the tragic divide within the beautiful region unfolds in all its brutal honesty. This artwork does not shy away from the distressing reality—of young and old lives lost to senseless violence, of the torment endured by the people of Kashmir. It tells of the unspeakable horrors—of women violated, their cries for help echoing in the chilling silence, and the rivers running red with the blood of the innocent. These horrors are painful, and they are real. Only a Kashmiri, one who has witnessed these dark times, can truly convey the depth of these truths.

In the canvas, we see a river, not serene and peaceful, but one stained with the blood of the fallen, a haunting symbol of the suffering that troubles this land. Boats drift aimlessly, carrying not passengers but the weight of anger and despair that has become all too familiar to the people of Kashmir. They have endured much, and their suffering is strongly felt. Every soul cries out for a solution and an end to the pain troubling their land. But the question remains, how can peace be achieved, and how can love be newly lit among neighbors who once shared their lives and culture?

The truth is, every problem has a solution, but it requires the willingness to seek a solution together. India and Pakistan continue to bear the burden of this conflict, and our hearts go out to the families who have suffered unthinkable loss.

To bring peace and love to the region, we must stop pointing fingers at each other and start reaching out in understanding. Once, these communities lived side by side, bound by shared histories and cultures. The dream of coexistence and rebuilding the bridges that have been broken, remains alive in the hearts of many.

May this artwork serve as a powerful reminder that it is within our collective power to bring peace to this land, to heal the wounds of Kashmir, and to foster a future where love, not hatred, prevails. Together, we can bring peace to this Mother Earth that we all share.

9. Title: *I Am Bangladeshi*
Medium: Acrylic
Size: 16x20
Date: 2.2.2021

Description: In this vibrant canvas, we celebrate the rich history of a young nation born from struggle and sacrifice. The declaration of Bangladesh's independence in March, 1971 marked the country's pivotal moment, an event whose 50th anniversary reminds us of the powerful, enduring spirit that birthed this new state and secured its hard-won freedom.

Settled on the northern coast of the Bay of Bengal, Bangladesh finds itself embraced by the powerful rivers of the Ganges and Brahmaputra. Its dynamic landscape is naturally marked by tropical monsoons, frequent floods, and cyclones, reflecting the constant environmental challenges faced by its people. Yet, despite this, the country has risen with strong determination.

The young kids portrayed in this painting serve as symbols of this youthful nation's hope and vitality. They show the spirit of a country flourishing and prospering despite its early struggles. The vibrant colors and the sense of freedom coming from this artwork capture the essence of Bangladesh's journey. This canvas reminds us that even in the face of hardship, its people have succeeded as a strong nation that stands tall on the global stage. As we look at these young faces, we see the future of Bangladesh, bright and promising, a statement to the unstoppable human spirit.

"I Am Bangladeshi" is a tribute to the rich history and enduring legacy of a nation that has overcome great odds. It is a reminder that freedom, once cherished, can lead to prosperity and growth. As the country continues to flourish, may its story serve as an inspiration to the world, showcasing the endless potential of a determined people.

10. Title: *Running for My Life*
Medium: Oil
Size: 30x30
Date: 2.18.08

Description: The backdrop of this painting is rooted in the aftermath of the Partition, a time when India and Pakistan had already been torn apart by conflict. I recount a deeply personal and traumatic experience from my childhood—an experience vividly illustrating the devastation of war on the innocent. However, the conflict cast its long shadow again, overwhelming the region in 1965 with an unforgiving chaos of violence and destruction.

I was just five years old when the drums of war began to beat. Our home was dangerously close to the border, which resulted in finding ourselves in the eye of the storm. Bombs fell from the skies while shelling, sirens and the frightening roar of airplanes filled the air as they launched their attacks. We had to blackout our windows at night and saw endless lines of tanks on the daytime streets.

The trauma of those days forced us to make a heart-breaking decision—to flee our town in search of safety. I, a small child, ran for my life, escaping the violence. This experience left me scarred, in body and in spirit. I carried the weight of post-traumatic stress, living in a constant state of fear and uncertainty, haunted by the belief that there was no safe place on this earth.

Reflecting on this painful memory, I cannot help but ask: When will we learn the lessons of our past? Why do wars persist, fueled by the unstoppable desires of those in power? Why must innocent lives be sacrificed in the pursuit of control? War does not solve problems; it only creates more suffering and destruction. It plunges us into darkness, robbing us of our humanity and leaving behind a trail of trauma and loss.

Running for My Life is not just a painting—it's a plea for peace. It's a call to those who abuse power to set aside their egos and ambitions and seek peaceful resolutions to conflicts. It's a reminder that no child or human being should endure the horrors of war, and that we must strive for a world where compassion and understanding triumph over the drums of war.

11. Title: Remember Us
Medium: Acrylic
Size: 16x20
Date: 10.16.2019

Description: In this piece we bear witness to a chapter of Partition that often goes unheard—a tale of abandonment and sorrow etched into the hearts of animals left behind, their silent cries echoing throughout the pages of history. 1947 marked the year when India declared independence from British rule, a time of great celebration and hope. Yet, beneath the surface of this monumental event, a profound tragedy unfolded—one that involved not only humans but also the innocent animals who shared their lives with them.

My father shared a story immortalized in his novel, "Peela Gulab" (Yellow Rose). He recounted how, in the days leading up to the division of the South Asia, the animals seemed to possess an inner understanding of the impending disaster. They stopped eating fresh grass, and the dogs began to howl, as if they knew what was to come. The heart-breaking moment arrived when my grandmother, faced with the unbearable decision of leaving behind her loyal animal companions, removed the ropes that bound them and told them to go, to flee to safety. But the animals, perhaps bound by an unspoken loyalty, stood still, tears in their eyes. My father, a witness to this devastating scene, never saw his beloved animals again.

This painting displays the tragedy that fell upon countless animals during the chaos after Independence. They look lost and sad, their world turned upside down by the circumstances of those times. The dust beneath their feet symbolizes the emptiness of abandonment, a reminder of a time when no one was there to care for them. The redrawing of the map uprooted millions of people, causing untold suffering and loss. It also left countless animals behind, their stories seldom told or remembered. My father's words, etched into this canvas, bear witness to their hardship.

"Remember Us" is a tribute to these forgotten souls, a powerful reminder of the bond that exists between humans and animals. It is an artwork that resonates with compassion and respect for the minds and hearts of animals who, in their own way, shared in the tragedy of that fateful divide. May it serve as a lasting statement to the importance of acknowledging the pain and suffering experienced by all living beings during times of turmoil.

150

12. Title: *Rooftop memories*
Medium: Acrylic
Size: 16x20
Date: 5.11.2022

Description: In many Asian countries, people love to fly kites from their rooftops. This is a special community activity where neighbors of all ages, from children to adults, gather to fly kites and compete. It's a joyful, shared experience built on rivalry and fun.

The biggest and most famous festival for this is Basant, which was historically celebrated across the entire region of unified Punjab. It was a huge tradition before the division of the land and continues to be honored today.

After the turning point of Independence, the Basant festival became a source of bittersweet memories. For those who were forced to leave their homes, the sight of kites flying now brings a deep sadness. It stirs up recollections of the good times spent with friends and neighbors they were never able to see again. The joy of the competition is forever mixed with the profound scar of separation.

152

13. Title: *Divided Rivers*
Medium: Acrylic
Size: 16x20
Date: 5.12.2022

Description: In this vivid canvas, we are confronted with the profound and painful story of Punjab, a land whose identity is woven into its very name: the "Land of Five Rivers." This name is derived from the Farsi words *Punj* ("five") and *Aab* ("water"), celebrating the flow of the five main tributaries— Sutlej, Beas, Ravi, Chenab, and Jhelum—which are the lifeblood of the entire region. Legend even holds that when the Mughal King Babur crossed these waters during his conquests, he declared his victory over the "Land of Five Waters." These rivers have shaped the history and culture of Punjab, and their importance runs deep in the hearts of its people.

The physical and emotional split of 1947 violently changed this unified landscape, creating East Punjab and West Punjab. While the country gained freedom, the land was torn in two. The old map, once whole and undivided, is now covered with bloody gauze. These pieces serve as a haunting reminder of the wounds inflicted upon the land and its people. These individuals, torn from their roots and labeled as refugees in their own land, suffered most from one of the most significant human disasters in world history. The price paid by these families was great, a terrible toll in exchange for the ultimate prize —freedom from British colonial rule. Partition left a scar on the shared memory of India.

My father once wisely noted, "It is a great idea never to be old," for the wounds of Partition run deep and serve as a reminder of the human cost of division. "Divided Rivers" is a heartfelt tribute to the strength of Punjab and its people, a powerful reminder of the scars that mark its history, and a plea for unity, understanding, and a future where the Five Rivers of the land flow together once more.

"During Partition, millions of innocent people died and millions were uprooted. I am one of them."
-Balbir Singh Momi (my Father)

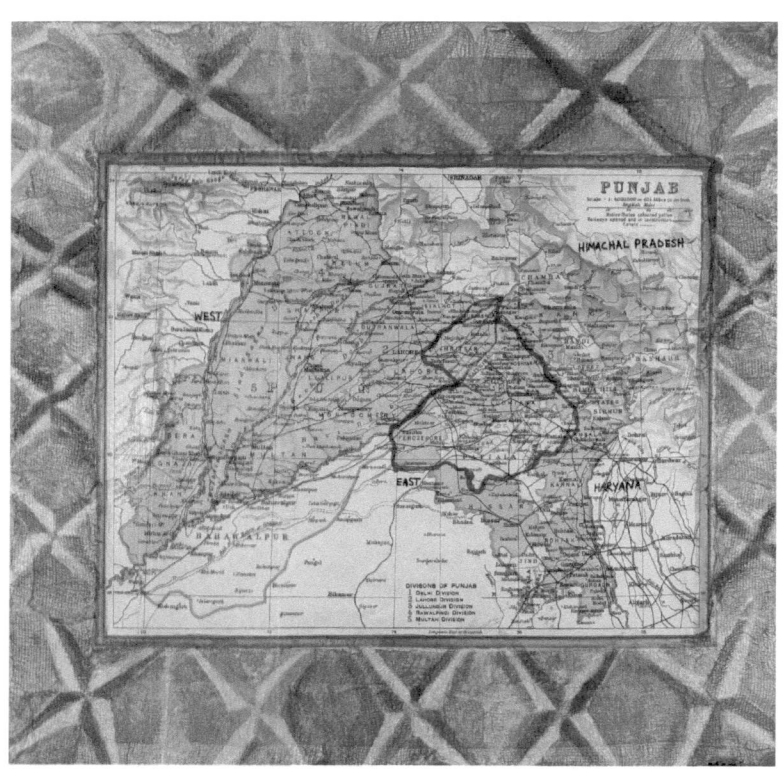

155

14. Title: *Where Are You From?*
Medium: Acrylic and Mixed Media
Size: 30x30
Date: 12.26.25

Description: The title is a question asked instinctively when one Punjabi meets another. It's never smalltalk, but a search for ancestry, memory, and belonging—a way to locate oneself through shared villages, surnames, rivers, and stories. This painting speaks to how refugees once asked the same question of each other, hoping to uncover a connection that could offer comfort amid loss.

At the center lies the image of undivided Punjab, shaped like a human heart—a vital organ now shrinking under the pressure of political history. The overlapping map of old and new borders reveals a tragic truth: the once-vast "Land of Five Rivers" is disappearing, sliced away by leaders who treat land like paper rather than heritage. Framing this shrinking and broken heart is a traditional Phulkari design in gauze, symbolizing the raw, unhealed trauma inflicted upon the body of the state. It serves as a haunting reminder that while maps may change, the soul of the land remains etched in the stories of those who were forced to leave it behind.

157

15. Title: *Looking Back 75 Years*
Medium: Acrylic
Size: 16x20
Date: 5.29.2022

Description: As we gaze at the canvas, we are transported to a profound moment in time—an emotional reflection on the passage of seven and a half decades. It is a moment of collective self-reflection, a journey into the heart and soul of both our nations. This piece was painted to commemorate 75 years since the creation of India & Pakistan—a lifetime for some, a blink in the grand sweep of history for others. Here, we reflect on the complex fabric of our shared existence.

We reflect on the profound losses, the absence of loved ones who live on only in our memories, and the homes left behind in pursuit of a new beginning.
We reflect on those who have passed away, their legacies etched in the stories they left behind.
We reflect on the living, whose courage have brought us to this moment.
We reflect on the pain—the emotional, the physical, the mental, and the financial—that has marked this journey.
We reflect on the land of our ancestors, a sacred bond that unites us all.
We reflect on the importance of not hating neighbors, dispelling rumors, and building bridges.
We reflect on our love for our homelands, our dedication to peace, and our commitment to kindness.
We promise not to let politicians sow division, for unity is our strength.

Together, we work to make our world a better place—one of love, peace, and kindness, where the echoes of the past guide us toward a brighter future.

A Trio On Canvas: How to End Suffering

A great rupture uprooted more than 20 million people, breaking apart families, shattering communities, and forever changing the landscapes of South Asia. The traumatic echoes of this event have endured across generations, shaping identities and histories. As an artist, I am compelled to give voice to these experiences—those of my parents, grandparents, and countless others who lived through this terrible event.

Unlike many narratives on 1947 that focus solely on violence and loss, my work also seeks to highlight strength, compassion, and healing. I focus on the untold stories of humanity that emerged in chaos—strangers offering refuge, communities uniting to protect the weak, and individuals rebuilding their lives from ashes.

My use of gauze as a medium is a deliberate choice, symbolizing both the wounds of Partition and the process of healing. The texture of gauze mirrors the layers of pain that must be addressed before scars can form, allowing audiences to feel both the rawness and the resilience of those who lived through this period.

The following three paintings work together: the first recognizes suffering, the second shows how to heal from it, and the third portrays the end of suffering. With that in mind, the viewer is invited to embark on a visual journey of practicing peaceful receiving.

16. Title: *Salima's Story*
Medium: Acrylic & Gauze
Size: 16x20
Date: 11.3.24

Description: The subject of this evocative painting, Salima Hashmi, spoke at an event I attended, where I had the opportunity to hear her touching story and later paint it:

"We left Srinagar on a bus," she recounted. "We were heading for Murree. I still remember it, at a place called Thrait: a bus full of massacred Sikhs. When we reached Murree, my mother organized a parade of women- a human attempt to stop the rioting and bloodshed. She sat me on a donkey and put a white flag in my hand. I was only a four-and-a-half-year-old. I was the leader, this tiny figure waving for peace. I scared of that donkey, but at the same time, felt this sense of pride, leading all those women."

Salima's Story is a statement to the power of compassion and courage, a call for a future built on peace and goodwill. In this vision, past and present merge, guiding us to a world where future generations live without borders, honoring the sacrifices of ancestors with enduring respect and empathy. Together, they represent a future generation's heartfelt desire for peace and connection with neighboring lands, honoring the places where their ancestors once lived in unity.

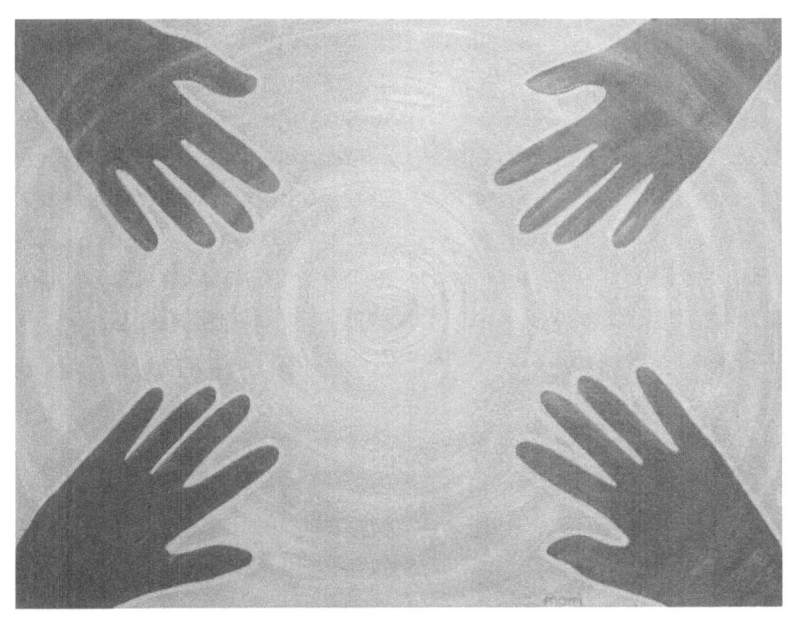

17. Title: *Healing Vibes*
Medium: Acrylic
Size: 16x20
Date: 11.5.2024

Description: This piece captures hands reaching out from all directions—East, West, North, and South. These hands are an expression of healing touch, of strength born from a shared humanity. Set against an invisible backdrop of struggle and separation, they remind us of the quiet moments when strangers extended compassion, moving across faith and background to heal and uplift one another. The painting celebrates the strength of collective kindness and the bonds that can rise even from deep pain. United hands symbolize a community of healing, a sanctuary from loss where compassion is sown. "Healing Vibes" inspires us to connect beyond divides, showing that even in suffering, we hold the power to heal each other and foster strength with unity.

18. Title: *New Future*
Medium: Acrylic
Size: 16x20
Date: 11.6.2024

Description: "New Future" depicts a blue sky filled with soaring white doves, symbolizing hope, unity, and peace. The remains of old structures lie below, embodying memories of a past shaken by the devastation of Partition. Yet, looking from this foundation, a positive future emerges, with each dove carrying messages of love and compassion for the generations to come. The painting evokes a sense of freedom and new beginnings, as communities rebuild from ashes, finding strength in solidarity. "New Future" reminds us that persistence is more than survival—it is the force that moves us toward a hopeful horizon, anchored in compassion and the will to rebuild.

This vision echoes across borders, bridging past and present, with a commitment to harmony and respect for the legacies of those who came before. Their ancestors' legacy of sacrifice finds new meaning in this act, as they call for a world where future generations will thrive in peace, understanding, and goodwill.

Notes for Reflecting on the Paintings

SECTION 3:
POETRY AS REMEMBRANCE

Inspired by my Father who drank water from all Five Rivers in Punjab.

Poems Dedicated to the Rivers of Punjab

The rivers of Punjab are more than just water — to us who have known them, they are living songs. Each one flows with its own rhythm, carrying stories of joy, sorrow, and belonging. They are magical & alive in their own way: rivers have melody, they change positions, their ends never meet. The Satluj, Beas, Raavi, Chenab, and Jhelum have shaped Punjab's heart and soul for centuries. They move and change, yet somehow stay connected — like family bound by memory.

From the earliest civilizations, the rivers have been the cradle of life. Mohenjo-Daro and the ancient cultures of the Indus Valley grew from their fertile banks, where water sustained not only the soil but also the spirit of human progress. For the farmers of Punjab, the rivers remain lifelines — nurturing fields of golden wheat and mustard, quenching the thirst of livestock, and blessing each harvest with renewal. Their flowing waters turn labor into abundance and keep the land breathing with life.

Beyond agriculture and ancient history, the rivers flow deep into the region's soul and literature. They are central characters in folklore and the tragic love stories that define Punjabi identity. Classic tales like *Heer Ranjha* and *Sohni Mahiwal* feature the waters as witnesses to passion, sorrow, and separation, with the Chenab River, in particular, becoming a symbol of ultimate, tragic love. Punjabi Sufi poets, such as Baba Farid and Bulleh Shah, used the river's endless current as a powerful metaphor for the spiritual journey, the ache of separation, and the search for the Divine. The rivers, therefore, do more than nourish the soil; they embody the shared human experience, carrying the memory of every joy and every grief across the divided land.

For our family, the rivers were part of life. My father learned to swim alongside animals in their waters. He drank from them, trusted them, and treated them as sacred. Many of our happiest days were spent by their banks — sharing food, laughter, and stories during long picnics in the sun.

Without these rivers, something in us would be missing. They gave music to our lives and meaning to our roots. These poems flow from that place — where beauty meets loss, and memory meets longing. They honor the rivers as living witnesses of Punjab's history — divided, yet still reaching for one another beneath the surface. By way of their endless song, the rivers remind us that even when separated, what was once united can never truly be torn apart.

1.
"The Tears of Punjab's Rivers"

In Punjab's heart, where rivers once did flow,
The Raavi, Jhelum, and Chenab, a tranquil show.
Satluj and Beas, a five-some so grand,
In Farsi's tongue, "Five Waters" in the land.
But fate unkind, 47's bitter toll,
Tore them apart, the rivers of the soul.
In tears they wept, their unity undone,
Five waters now divided, forever on the run.

2.
"Raavi's Sorrow"

Raavi, the queen of the northern expanse,
Once danced freely, in a joyful trance.
Now split by borders, a silent cry,
Her tears in the night reach for the sky.
As she flows alone, a solo grace,
She longs for the touch of her sister's embrace.
Separated by land, they share a heart,
In Raavi's everlasting flow, they never part.

3.

"Jhelum's Song"

Jhelum, once a melody, now sighs,
Her gentle waves reflect the skies.
Through ancient valleys she used to roam,
Now quieter waters call her home.
Still in her depths, old stories stay,
Of love once near, now far away.
She hums a tune of what's been lost,
Yet carries on — no matter the cost.

4.

"Chenab's Whispers of Unity"

Chenab, the lifeblood of a vibrant land,
Met with division, a fate unplanned.
She may be split and her waters apart,
But in the depths of her soul, a hopeful heart.
Chenab's flow, a reminder of love's embrace,
Her waters, a whisper, of what time can't erase.

5.
"Satluj and Beas, Together Forever"

Satluj and Beas still flow as one,
Rivers untouched when new borders were spun.
By fields of gold their waters glide,
Yet sorrow drifts along their side.
For they remember what others lost—
The silent cries, the painful cost.
Their sisters, parted by lines of fate,
Left stories the waters still resonate.
So they keep moving, soft and slow,
Carrying echoes wherever they go.
Satluj and Beas, in steady stream,
Guarding the past like a fragile dream.

6.

"The River's Promise"

By the water's edge, we found our way,
In the Land of Five Rivers, where we used to play.
But when they parted, our hearts did ache,
Yet the rivers still flow, a new path they make.

Oh, Land of Five Rivers, we'll mend the divide,
In your name, we'll stand side by side.
Once we were torn, we will heal, we will grow,
For the Land of Five Rivers, love will always show.

Poems on the Chaos After Independence

If rivers embody the everlasting spirit and hope of the region, these poems capture the deep, enduring human cost of their division. This collection moves from the geographical split to the raw, personal inheritance of pain, charting the journey of millions who suddenly found themselves labeled refugees. These poems bear witness to the unspeakable violence and chaos that erupted on that fateful day—the tragedy of the displacement, the desperate conditions of the refugee camps, and the heartbreaking loyalty of the innocent animals left behind. Most importantly, these poems confront the unseen trauma; the generational burden of sorrow and displacement that continues to shape families today. They serve as a record of the collective wounds that were inflicted, demanding recognition, remembrance, and action so that the memory of what was lost can finally lead to healing.

1.
"Echoes of '47"

Bloodshed and sorrow, our stories entwined,
The division's scars still haunt our minds.
Powerless we were, in our own homeland,
With nothing but grief, we tried to understand.
No therapy to heal, just memories of the past,
In '47, a nightmare that forever lasts.

2.

"The Refugees' Tale"

Refugees in our land, a bitter twist of fate,
The dawn of two nations, we carried the burden of our state.
No homes, no beds, no dishes, just despair,
In a land divided, we found pain everywhere.
Animals left behind, neighbors torn apart,
Relatives and friends, lost with heavy hearts.
Disease spread in camps, where death was near,
No comfort or relief, the struggle for life was dear.

3.
"The Unseen Trauma"

The year of Independence, millions of souls,
Thrown into a future out of control.
Over two million lives cruelly snatched away,
As we became refugees on that fateful day.
No food, no money, no land to till,
In this new world, powerless still.
Strangers to each other, in a land divided
The promise of freedom was deeply misguided.

4.
"The Suffering of Hearts"

In '47, our emotions held the weight,
As we silently suffered in a divided state.
No peace, no comfort, just a heartache profound,
In the echoes of that year, our souls are still bound.
Seventy-plus years may have passed us by,
But the pain of that date still makes us cry.
Let us remember the bloodshed, the trauma we bore,
In the hope that one day, peace will restore.
Oh, India and Pakistan, let's bridge the divide,
With peace and friendship, we shall stand side by side.
In unity and love, we will rewrite the story,
Seventy-plus years now, let's imagine the glory.
From Lahore to Delhi, from Karachi to Mumbai,
Our shared heritage is calling, beneath the same sky.
Let's cherish the cultures that make us unique,
So the deep bond between us may now speak.
No more borders, no more pain,
Let's heal the wounds, break the chain.
Hand in hand, we will face the strife,
And all together, we will embrace a new life.
In the name of progress, let's come together,
For our children's future, for peace forever.
We have shared history and we have shared tears,
Now let's share joy, and lose our fears.
As the sun sets on the past, a new era begins,
For peace to be shared, let our kinship win.
Seventy-plus years, but it's not too late,
For peace and friendship, let's celebrate

Poems Based on My Paintings

The following poems were born from my original paintings, translating the visual language of color, texture, and form into the narrative rhythm of poetry. This work would not have been possible without the in-depth conversations I had with my parents. As their child, I listened to their stories on culture, food, music, their animals, the belongings left behind, and a vision formed. I experienced and ultimately created this work through my parents' words.

This collection is an act of deep remembrance, bringing together art, literature, and culture to explore the profound sorrow and memories of 1947. Where the paintings give tangible form to the unseen trauma, the poems give voice to their silent stories.

These pieces serve as powerful reminders not to forget. They are designed to educate the reader by revealing the human history told in every brushstroke and every line. Together, this fusion of art and poetry creates a space to witness, to process the stories of our ancestors, and to finally begin to heal.

1.

"My Dad's Hope" (Based on One Day We Will be One Again)

"My daughter," he says, "may we unite once more,
No need for Partition, let peace restore.
We have lost so much in this divide,
Can we heal our wounds and stand by each side?
Our great grandparents, with hearts full of pain,
Left with a void, an everlasting strain.
What can the next generation do,
To mend our trauma, to build anew?
To be good neighbors, as we once were,
In a land of unity, where love did stir.
Division can't make us bitter or cold,
For our shared history, let our hearts unfold.
Stories from both sides, they resonate,
A tale of love, it's never too late.
My father took us to Lahore one day,
To see my mom's house, where she used to play.
The whole neighborhood came to greet our kin,
Like years of distance had never set in.
In her home, emotions flowed in tears,
Such great reception, it calmed our fears.
People longed to see their loved ones again,
Separated by borders, by sorrow and pain.
So many lost, in different camps they would roam,
But in their hearts, they longed for home.
In this painting, flags of India and Pakistan merge,
A vision of unity, let our hearts converge.
Only writers and artists, with love they see,
A world of compassion, where all can be free.

Food, art, and music, they hold the key,
To bring people together, in harmony.
It may not happen soon, but we can dream,
Of a world reunited, in love's gentle stream.

2.

"Running for My Life"

"Running for My Life," the story unfolds,
A plea for peace, for war to be controlled.
In a world where innocence should thrive,
A child's nightmare, just trying to survive.
At five years old, by India and Pakistan's borders,
A war erupted, from military orders.
Bombs falling from a darkened sky,
Shelling and airplanes, peace denied.
A town once safe, became a battleground,
Innocence lost, in the thundering sound.
A child's eyes witnessed a world ablaze,
In the midst of chaos, a fearful maze.
Forced to leave, to escape the fight,
A child's world now full of fright.
PTSD's shadow, it lingered on,
As if there was no safe place to dawn.
No child, no human, should know the pain,
Of war's unending, destructive rain.
When will these men with egos vain,
Stop feeding fire for their personal gain?
War, a cruel dance, it does not solve,
It shatters lives, humanity's resolve.
It takes us backward, it leaves a scar,
Killing innocent souls, no matter how far.
In "Running for My Life," a plea we make,
For peace to be, for war's grip to break.
May leaders heed, and hatred cease,
So every child's heart can find its peace.

3.
"Innocent Eyes Left Behind"

Innocent eyes, left unattended, they stare,
Faithful creatures, hearts heavy with despair.
Owners had to leave, for their safety's sake,
But these loyal souls, left with hearts that ache.
Three days without fresh grass to feed,
In their silence, a story takes seed.
Animals sensed trouble in the air,
Nature warned them of a deep despair.
Dogs howled at the sky, as if they knew,
The coming turmoil, a terrifying view
When the day came, for the family's departure,
Tears welled in eyes, a silent fracture.
Ropes removed, a command gently spoken,
"Go away," their hearts, deeply broken.
Yet they didn't move, their trust unchanging,
In their eyes, tears of sorrow, love remaining.
My dad's story, a powerful retelling,
Of a time when hearts were deeply dwelling.
Innocent animals, lost in the divide,
Their faithful companions, no longer by their side.
In this painting, their crisis laid bare,
Lost and sad, with nobody to care.
The dust underfoot tells a tale untold,
Of innocence left behind, in a world so cold.
Countless animals, too, in their distress,
A shared story, in the darkest recess.
"Innocent Eyes Left Behind," we cherish them here,
The creatures who suffered, their tale we hold dear.

SECTION 4: THE ONGOING CRISIS

Introduction

As we reflect on the historical events that shaped our region and examine the enduring impact of the past, we acknowledge that history is a living narrative, influenced by present-day occurrences. In light of recent developments that resonate deeply with the themes explored in this book, I have included two extra chapters that go in-depth into the context and cause of this new event. These chapters aim to connect our understanding of history with contemporary experiences, highlighting the ongoing relevance of our stories. Finally, I end the section with an open letter to the reader, posing the uncomfortable questions about the legacy of the events of 1947 that remain unasked & unresolved.

I

Who Controls Punjab's Rivers?

The question of who controls Punjab's rivers is a deeply complicated and politically charged one that lies at the very heart of Punjab's relationship with the Central Government in Delhi. Control over these vital water resources has been a persistent source of conflict, with the disputes beginning as early as the reorganization of states after Partition.

The process of officially removing control from the river state —Punjab—began in 1966. Following the creation of Haryana and Himachal Pradesh, the Central Government established the Bhakra Management Board (BMB) under the Punjab Reorganisation Act. This legislative act immediately transferred major projects like the Bhakra Dam out of the sole control of the Punjab State Government. The full transfer was completed in 1976 with the creation of the Bhakra Beas Management Board (BBMB). This Centre-administered board took over the Pong Dam and the Beas-Sutlej link. Since then, the BBMB has regulated the supply of water and power, not just to Punjab, but also to "partner states," including non-river regions like Rajasthan and Delhi. This means the Central-controlled BBMB has managed the flow of these rivers for nearly five decades.

The foundation for this central control was laid even earlier with the Indus Waters Treaty (IWT) of 1960. This treaty with Pakistan was a foundational political act that assigned the waters of the Eastern Rivers (Raavi, Beas, and Sutlej) to India for exclusive use. This needed a master plan to harness these rivers for irrigation and power across the wider Northern plains. For Punjab, this was a fundamental rerouting of their natural, historic water flow to serve the needs of other regions, permanently altering the state's ecology and hydrology.

The argument that this control has led to mismanagement is supported by several ongoing issues and legislative actions. The Punjab Reorganisation Act, 1966, remains the legal basis for the current system, transferring control to a board where non-river states gained a share of Punjab's water assets. This disregard for local river rights is clearest in the constant water sharing disputes, where Punjab's objections are often overruled by the votes of non-river members within the BBMB. Furthermore, the political pressure to complete the Sutlej-Yamuna Link (SYL) Canal is seen as a hostile attempt to take the state's natural resources, fueling the claim that the Centre is acting against Punjab's interests.

Beyond the political disputes, there is the devastating issue of operational failures. Recurring, severe floods have frequently been labeled a man-made disaster by local political leaders and experts. The primary allegation is that dam authorities fail to follow standard "rule curves" — the protocols for gradually releasing water before the monsoon season — which results in sudden, massive discharges during heavy rains that flood downstream areas. Stakeholders also complain that the BBMB's operations are "totally opaque," limiting access to real-time information necessary for local flood preparation. Finally, the 2022 amendments to the BBMB Rules, which removed the requirement that key members be nominated from Punjab and Haryana, have been widely opposed as a legislative move to further centralize control and "attack the federal structure" of the country.

The belief that this control has led to mismanagement is sustained by giving water rights to states that don't border the rivers, numerous disputes over how to share the water, and clear failures in managing the dams during floods.

Pause for a Moment's Reflection

II

What was the Cause of the August 2025 Flooding in Punjab?

On August 14, 2025, as the Sutlej swallowed Punjab's villages, the cries of the people rose louder than the rain. Families clung to rooftops, livestock floated in the brown waters, and fields of rice and wheat—the year's lifeline—were erased overnight. Yet from Delhi, there was silence. This chapter is an in-depth effort by the author to bring clarity to this tragedy that seems destined to be pushed under the rug and forgotten.

Relentless monsoon rains pounded the Punjab region for four days straight without pause, swelling the Sutlej River beyond its banks. Both India and Pakistan felt the fury as floodwaters surged through the villages lying close to the river. In dozens of villages, homes were submerged, forcing families to flee with little more than the clothes on their backs. More than 600 villages across both Indian and Pakistani Punjab were drowned in muddy waters.

The tragedy was immediate and absolute. Thousands of acres of crops—rice, wheat, sugarcane, and cotton—were lost, destroying the livelihoods of countless farmers just weeks before harvest across 120,000 hectares of cropland. Nearly 15,000 head of livestock—buffalo, goats, and cows that were the very lifeline of rural families—passed away in the currents, cutting off not only food sources but the very backbone of their economies. Human deaths mounted as some were swept away by currents while others succumbed to disease and lack of shelter in the aftermath. At least 75,000 people were forced to abandon their homes, seeking shelter in makeshift camps.

The devastation did not stop at the border. The Sutlej River, flowing from India into Pakistan, carried the destruction downstream, making the suffering collective. Floods do not respect political lines; they carve suffering equally on both sides. In both Indian and Pakistani Punjab, families stood on rooftops, watching helplessly as ancestral homes collapsed into the flood. The floods left scars on the land and hearts of Punjab. Fields that once promised life now spoke the silence of devastation.

This disaster was not an unforeseen act of God, but a predictable, man-made disaster engineered by years of long-term failure from the hostile, faraway power in Delhi. It was a tragedy born from cold disregard, with echoes of a pattern of oppression felt repeatedly by the Punjabi people.

The true cause was the disastrous, poorly timed release of water from Centre-controlled upstream dams. For days, the Bhakra, Pong, and Ranjit Sagar dams held water at dangerously high levels, creating immense pressure. Despite clear forecasts of heavy rainfall, the authorities—managed again not locally as was the historical case but by the Centre-controlled Bhakra Beas Management Board (BBMB)—refused to release water gradually and in advance. Instead, when the monsoon rains reached their peak, the gates were thrown open, unleashing a devastating surge directly onto an already overwhelmed Punjab. Political leaders across party lines publicly criticized this action, labeling it "criminal negligence" rather than an act of God. They questioned why the dams were not managed to hold the surplus water, asking directly: Why was the water not released gradually in advance, so that the dams could later hold the extra water? Had it been done on time, the extent of devastation could have been less.

The political decision-making was worsened by complete collapse of utilities and physical systems meant to keep rising waters in check. The crashing of two floodgates at the Madhopur Dam in Pathankot was not an accident of nature; it was a physical manifestation of poor maintenance and neglect, directly contributing to the flooding of large areas of the Gurdaspur and Pathankot districts. This decay in inner networks—the canals left clogged, the riverbanks left unreinforced—was the result of years of resources focused on emergency response rather than prevention.

Across the border, the accusation was even sharper. Pakistani officials, citing releases into the Sutlej, Raavi, and Chenab rivers, immediately accused India of "using water as a weapon" and deliberately causing wide-scale flooding in their

199

territory. This international accusation further put forward the perception that the disaster was not an accident, but the consequence of a government that views Punjab's resources and safety through a lens of political control and indifference. The Sutlej tragedy of 2025 was the latest, most bitter price paid for being governed by an authority that prioritizes politics over people.

The size of the 2025 event can only be fully understood by reviewing past disasters. The numbers provide a realistic baseline of the region's exposure to these events. The 2019 Punjab floods that followed heavy rains led to the flooding of around 700 villages in Indian Punjab, forcing the evacuation of 50,000+ people and the loss of thousands of livestock, with crop damage stretching across 100,000 hectares (mainly rice, cotton, maize). The scale of the 2025 flood was a chilling echo of the horrifying 2022 Pakistan floods that affected 33 million people nationwide, caused over 1,700 deaths, and saw 1.2 million livestock killed across the country, with hundreds of villages underwater in Punjab province alone. These previous events provided clear warnings that went unheard.

In the immediate aftermath of the August 2025 disaster, the response was delayed and uneven, laying bare the priorities of the state.

In India, the National Disaster Response Force (NDRF) and Army units were deployed to rescue stranded families and provide food, water, and medicine. The government declared a state of emergency in the worst-affected districts, authorizing the NDRF and Army to work alongside state authorities. Helicopters dropped food packets, while boats ferried stranded families to safety. In past floods (2019, 2021), central government financial aid packages were announced for Punjab farmers whose crops were lost.

In Pakistan, the Provincial Disaster Management Authority (PDMA), NGOs like the Edhi Foundation, and international groups such as UNICEF and the Red Crescent mobilized aid. Organizations like Khalsa Aid worked across borders, bringing food, medical care, and rebuilding support to families in distress.

Yet, despite the official statements and emergency responses, critics argued that words came faster than action. The political symbolism of aerial surveys and press releases was cold comfort to those survivors waiting in relief camps for basics like food, medicine, and clean drinking water. Many families understood that community kitchens served quicker than government kitchens.

No leader came to stand with Punjab. No promise of hope echoed from the capital. To many, it felt as if the suffering of Punjabis was not an accident of nature alone, but also the result of a government that chose not to see them. Yet, it was the people themselves who carried each other through.

Gurdwaras across Punjab opened their doors, cooking *langar* day and night for the displaced, while NGOs like Khalsa Aid and local farmer unions organized boats, blankets, and medicines. International Sikh diaspora groups sent funds and supplies, reminding Punjab that its strength comes not from rulers, but from its own spirit of solidarity. The floods did not only drown villages—they exposed the deep wounds between the state and its people. Punjab survived, but not because of

Delhi. Punjab survived because Punjabis refused to let each other die.

The response to the August 2025 floods was an extension of a powerful, historic pattern of self-reliance and community action. This was evident during the 2019 Punjab floods in India, when singers like Gurdas Maan, Sidhu Moosewala, Diljit Dosanjh, Harbhajan Mann, and others donated money and campaigned for relief, and again during the 2022 Pakistan floods, where Punjabi singers and actors on both sides raised funds through concerts and social media campaigns. Throughout these crises, the Sikh diaspora abroad—especially in Canada, UK, and USA—collected millions through *gurdwaras* and community groups, cementing their vital role.

The celebrity response this time was unparalleled. Over 25 Punjabi singers and actors came forward to adopt villages, pledging to rebuild homes, schools, and *gurdwaras*. Big names like Diljit Dosanjh, Gurdas Maan, Ammy Virk, and Neeru Bajwa called on their fans worldwide to donate, effectively turning concerts into fundraisers. Gurdas Maan, the legend of Punjabi music, pledged support for farmers and sang, "*Punjab da dil kabhi nahi doobda*" (Punjab's heart never sinks). Diljit Dosanjh donated *crores*, adopted villages, and rallied his global fanbase across Canada, the UK, and America. Ammy Virk visited relief camps, lifted morale with his songs, and funded the rebuilding of schools. Even though he was gone, Sidhu Moosewala's legacy lived on as his family and fans worldwide raised money in his name. Harbhajan Mann organized concerts to channel funds back into Punjab, while Neeru Bajwa adopted a cluster of villages, focusing specifically on women and children.

Other significant contributors included Karan Aujla, Sharry Mann, Sunanda Sharma, and Nimrat Khaira, each pledging *lakhs* of rupees and urging fans to stand for Punjab, and Babbu Maan who helped rebuild homes in the rural Malwa belt. Punjabi diaspora icons like Jazzy B and Garry Sandhu sent funds and visited flood-hit areas.

Actors and public figures also threw their weight behind the recovery. Sonam Bajwa provided medical kits and sanitary supplies for women in relief camps. Jimmy Shergill supported housing projects for displaced families. Cricketers Harbhajan Singh and Yuvraj Singh used their foundations and resources to supply food packets and medical relief, with Yuvraj specifically sending aid through his NGO YouWeCan. Within weeks, the Punjabi community raised over ₹200 crores (around $25 million USD) through *gurdwaras*, charities, and diaspora donations. Diaspora Sikhs from Canada, the UK, and America sent tractors, medical supplies, and direct cash to families in need.

Each adopted village received not just money, but human presence—artists visiting camps, singing for children, and promising farmers that Punjab would stand again. Most of all, the strength came from ordinary Punjabis: farmers who lost their own crops still helped neighbors clear fields; women cooked *langar* in makeshift kitchens day and night; and young men formed volunteer rescue teams, using tractors as boats to pull people from floodwaters.

The message was clear: Punjab survives not because of Delhi, but because Punjabis refuse to give up. Their spirit, their songs, and their solidarity are stronger than any flood. Punjab will be stronger than before, they will rebuild a new land of spirituality and strength. My best wishes to every Punjabi: you are a survivor now and The Land of Gold will come back stronger than before.

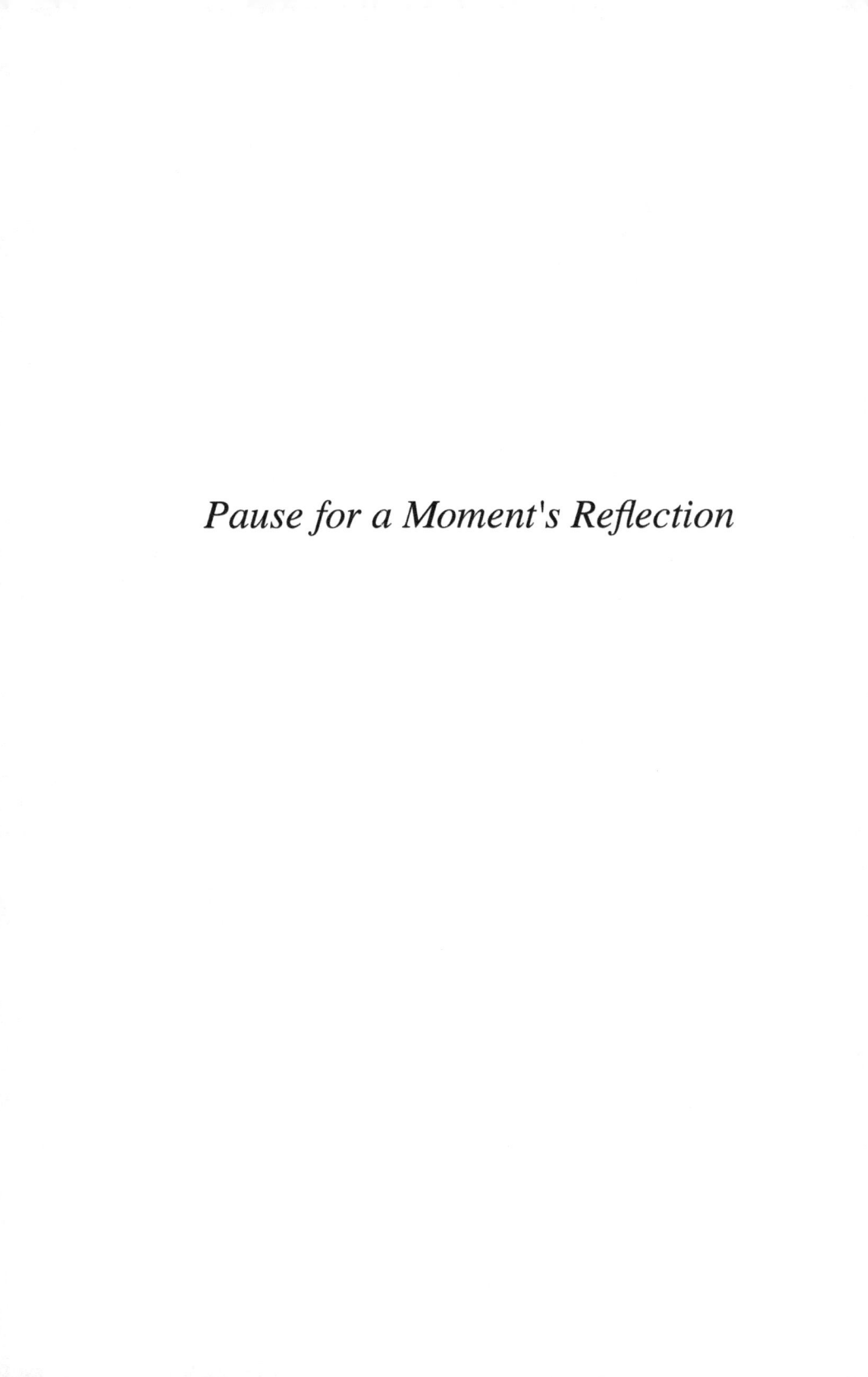

Pause for a Moment's Reflection

An Open Letter to the Reader

How long are we going to fight?

Seventy-plus years have passed since the Partition of India and Pakistan, yet the wounds remain fresh, etched into the minds of generations. What began as a rushed political decision cloaked in fear has left behind a legacy of bitterness, violence, and mistrust. We ask—how long are we going to fight over borders drawn by those who never truly knew our people, our languages, or our dreams?

How long are we going to allow injustice to fester?

The injustice did not end in 1947. It continued in the form of displacement, exclusion, and unresolved trauma. Those millions who lost their homes, their loved ones, and their identities—many dying nameless deaths, their stories remain buried under silence. To this day, neither government has offered a formal apology, nor have proper memorials been built to honor the lives lost. When will we acknowledge their pain as part of our shared responsibility?

How long are we going to kill innocent civilians?

Innocent lives are still caught in the crossfire of political rivalry—along the borders, in disputed territories, and through cycles of communal unrest. Every shell fired, every child orphaned, every family torn apart is a haunting echo of Partition's unfinished business. Are we truly so blinded by our politics that we cannot see the humanity on the other side?

How long are we going to suffer—and place suffering on others?

The trauma of 1947 lives on in every refugee story, every missing family member, and every unanswered glance across the barbed wire. But we do not suffer alone—we have passed down that pain to the next generation. Why are we still raising our children with suspicion, teaching them to remember only the enemy and not the shared history of music, poetry, and language that once connected us?

How long will we live under the shadow of "divide and rule"?

We inherited this system from our colonial past, and yet we have embraced it in our own politics. Religion, caste, and region continue to be used as weapons to divide us. When will we realize that the true cost of the rupture was not just physical separation, but the emotional and spiritual breaking apart of a people once bound by soil and song?

When are we going to stop blaming each other?

For decades, we have pointed fingers, rewritten history, and clung to nationalist narratives. But where has that blame gotten us? Our shared sorrow deserves more than blame—it deserves reflection. A divided past cannot build a united future unless both sides are willing to accept their roles and seek common ground.

When are we going to stop fighting for thrones?

Political power has too often been prioritized over human life. Leaders on both sides have taken advantage of fear, using national wounds to win votes and silence dissent. Are thrones worth more than the lives of our people? What kind of leadership is it that thrives only when its citizens are taught to hate?

Have we learned our lessons yet?

If we had, perhaps our borders would be softer, our dialogues more open, and our memories less bitter. Perhaps we would teach our children about coexistence, not conquest; about peaceful acceptance, not revenge. Perhaps we would honor the pain of the division of the land by ensuring such a thing never happens again.

History gave us a hard lesson in 1947. But history is not finished. It is written every day, by our choices, our silences, and our voices. The question is no longer what Partition did to us. The question is: what are we doing with its legacy?

It is time—to heal, to listen, to remember, and to rise above what broke us. The subcontinent cannot afford another seventy-plus years of pain. The time for unity, empathy, and collective appraisal is now. Let peace begin with us.

With all my love,

Tanya Momi

Pause for a Moment's Reflection

SECTION 5: A TRIBUTE

A Letter Across Time

By Balbir Singh Momi

In 1961, fourteen years after the tragic events of 1947, my father returned to his ancestral home in Pakistan—a place written into his soul and his many published works, even after being forced to leave it behind as a young man. After that visit, he wrote a letter to his own father, pouring out the heartbreak and longing stirred by walking once again through the rooms of a life interrupted. On June 21, 2024, I, his daughter, asked him to recreate that letter—to put into words what memory and silence had carried for decades.

This letter is not just a recollection: it is grief folded into words; the voice of a son standing in a home that once echoed with laughter that now hummed with absence. He told me he went back to Pakistan seven times, sleeping in his childhood room six of those visits. He searched for the animals they left behind during the hurried, painful migration—hoping to find something familiar had survived and somehow part of his past was still alive. But they were gone.

He thought often about bringing his parents back to see the home. But he knew the emotional toll would be too much. So he chose to go alone, to carry the weight for them. He used to say, *"I don't know why I longed for home so much—it didn't even make sense."* And yet, that longing never left him.

This English version of his letter preserves the rawness, the memory, and the aching love he held for a home he could never truly return to. It is a son's quiet conversation with his father across time and loss—a reflection of all that Partition tore apart, and all that still lives in the hearts of those who remember.

ਸਤਿਕਾਰ - ਯੋਗ ਸਿਘ ੨੭੮, ਸ਼੍ਰੋਮ ਸੈਲ੍ਹੂ ਪਟਾ (ਪਾਟਿਆਲਾ)
ਸੈਕਟ (੧੦।

ਪਿਆਰੇ ਬਾਪੂ ਜੀ
ਮੈਂ ਇਹ ਚਿੱਠੀ ਆਪਣੇ ਪ੍ਰਾ ਹਿੱਤ੨ਮ ਦੇ੨ ਪਿੱ੨ ੨ ਆਪ ਪਤੇ ਅਾ
...

New Village, Chak No. 78
District Sheikhupura, Pakistan
November 1961

Page 1

Dear *Bapu* (Father) *Ji* (Term of respect),
I am writing to you from our ancestral home, in our village here in Pakistan. I have been staying for several days now. A man named Chaudary Nazeem Ahmed & his family were allotted our property. He is a very kind man and has welcomed me warmly—he's told me I can stay as long as I like—but insists I don't eat food from outside; everything must come from their kitchen only.

I have met many people from the village — Grace, who used to clear the cow dung, Haleem, her son; Jivan the oil-pressor, Ramzan the postman, and many others from who remember you from your time in the village. They all remember you fondly and cry when they think of you over and over again.

The house remains as it was. Time seems to have paused here. Nothing has changed. Even the school looks exactly the same. The old primary school was destroyed in a flood, and a new one has not been built yet—so now, all the younger students are taught in the larger school building.

The elders of the village remember you fondly. They speak of you often, with deep affection. They wish you could return, if only to meet the Muslim families who came from India and now live here. These new residents are good people—gentle souls who miss their own homes across the border in India.

The orchards—some small, some grand—have been replanted. But they feel empty and abandoned, stripped of the vibrance and beauty they once we held. The people are friendly, and many express sorrow about what happened in 1947. "If Pakistan had to be made," they say, "then why did people have to be uprooted like this?"

There is no *Gurdwara* here anymore. It has been turned into a mosque. The larger, historical *Gurdwaras* have been preserved, but the smaller ones have either been demolished or converted into homes. No new homes are built, and they don't even repair the old. The biggest reason for that is the new families don't seem settled. They move from place to place, lost and still searching for something they may never find.

ਯਾਤਰੂਆਂ ਦੀ ਦਸ਼ਾਂ

ਇਹ ਆਖਦੇ ਧਾਰਤਰਾਂ ਤੇ ਸ਼ਿਲੇਵਰਾਂ ਨੂੰ ਕਰਨੇ ਨਾ ਵਿਚ
ਹੋਣਾ ਰਾਮ ਕੋਰ ਪੁਰਤੇਰੀਆਂ ਸਾਂਯ ਹੋ ਰਹੀ ਸਾ ਰਹੇ ਸੀ
ਰੀ ਬੋਸਰ ਕੋਰ ਪੁਰਤੇਰੀਆਂ ਸਾਂਯ ਵਿਚ ਹੀ ਯਾਰਲੇ ਸਾਰ ਰਹਾ
ਪੁਰਤੇਰੀਆਂ ਸਾਂਯ ਕਰ ਪੁਰਤੇਰੀਆਂ ਯਾਰਤਾਂ ਸਦੇਰਮਾ ਰੇਹੀ
ਰਰ ਰੇ ਦਿਰਾਂ ਸਾਰ ਯੂਰੀ ਕੀ ਰੇਰੀਆਂ ਨੇ ਇਹ ਕੀਨੇ ਵਿਰ
ਵਾਮਾਮਰਮ ਸਰੀਸੀਰੀ ਰਹੇ ਵ ਰਹੇ ਵ ਰਿਕੀਆਂ ਰਹਾ ਰੇਰੀ ਯਰਤੋਰ
ਪਰਮਲੇ ਧਾਰਤੇ ਨੂੰ ਯਾਰਰ ਰੇਰ ਯਰਰ ਕਰੇਰੀ ਰੇਰ ਰਰਨਾ
ਰਹੂ ਰੇ ਕੀਨੇ ਇਹ ਰੇ ਕੀਨੇ ਰਹਾ ਯਰਤੋਰ ਰਾ ਕੀਨੇ ਰਹੂ ਰੇ
ਪੁਰਕੀਰਾ ਰੇ ਰਾਰਰਾਰਾ ਰਰ ਰੇ ਰੇਰਾ ਰੇਰਾ ਰਹਾ ਰਹੇ ਕੀਨੇ ਨੂੰ
ਰੂ ਰਰ ਰਹਾ ਯਰ ਰ ਯਾਰਰਾਰ ਰੇਰਰਾ ਰੇ ਯਰ ਰਹਾ ਕੀਨੇ
ਯੂਰਰ ਇਹ ਰੇ ਯਰਰੇ ਰੇਰ ਰਹਰ ਰਾਮ ਯਾ ਰੇ ਰਾ ਰਰਾ ਯਰਰਾ
ਇਹ ਰਾ ਰੇਰਰ ਰੇਰ ਰਰਰਾ ਰਰੇ ਰੇ ਰਰ ਰਾਮ ਰੇ ਰੇ ਯੁਰਾਰੇ ਕੀਨੇ ਨੇ ਨੂੰ ਯਾਰ
ਰੇ ਰਰ ਰਾਰਰੇ ਰਰਰ ਰੇ ਰਰਾ ਯਰਰ ਰੇ ਰਰੇ ਰਹਰ ਰਾਮ
ਰਾਰ ਰੇਰ ਯਰ ਰੇਰ ਯਾਰਰਾਰ ਰੇ ਯਾਰ ਕੀਨੇ ਰੇ ਰਹ ਕੀਨੇ
ਰਾਰਰ ਰੇਰਾ ਰ ਰਾਰਰਾ ਰ ਰਾਰ ਰਾ ਰ ਰਰੀ ਰਾਰ ਰਰ ਰਰ
ਪੁਰਤੇਰੀ ਰੇ ਯ ਰਾਰ ਰੇਰ ਰੇ ਯਾਰਰੇ ਰੇ ਯਾਰਰੇ ਕੀਨੇ ਰਰਾ
ਰਰ ਰੇ ਰਰਾ ਪੁਰਾਰੇਯਾਂ ਯਰ ਯਾਰ ਰੇ ਯਾਰਰੇ ਰਾ ਰੇ ਰੁਰ
ਰਾਰ ਰਰੇ ਰਰਾ

ਰਾ ਰੇ ਰਾ ਯਰ ਯੁਰਰ ਰੇਰ ਰੇਰਰ ਰੇ ਰੇ ਯਰ ਯੇ ਰਾ ਰਾ
ਰੇਰਰੀ ਰੇਰਰਾ ਯਾਰੇਰਰੀ ਸਾਂਯ ਰਹੇ ਯਾਰਰੇ ਰੇਰੇ ਯਾਰਾ ਰੇਰੀ
ਰਰੇ ਰਾਰਰਰਾ ਰਾ ਰੇਰ ਰੇ ਰੇਰਰੇਰਾਰਰਰ ਰੇਰੇ ਰੇਰੇ
ਰਰਰਾਂ ਰੇ ਯਾਰਰ ਰਰ ਰੇ ਯੇ ਯਾਰੀਰੇਰਾ ਰਰ ਰੇ ਰਰ ਯਰਰ
ਯਰਰ ਰੇ ਯਾਰ ਰਰਰੇ ਰਰਾ ਰਾ ਰਰ ਯ ਰਿਰਾਰਰ ਰੇਰਾ ਰੇ ਯਾਰ
ਯਰ ਰੇ ਰਰ ਰੇਰ ਯ ਰੇ ਯਾ ਰਾ ਯੁਰਾਰੇ ਰਿਰਾਂ ਰੇ ਰਾ ਰਾਮ
ਰੇਰਰ ਯਰ ਰੇ ਯਾਰ ਰੇ ਰਿਰਾਯਰੀ
ਰੇ ਰਿਰਾਂ ਰ ਰਿਰ ਯਾਰ ਰਰ ਰੀ ਯੁਰੇਰ ਰਿਰੀ ਰੇਰਰ ਰੇ
ਵੀ ਰਾਂ ਇਹ ਰਾ ਰਰਾ ਯਾਰ ਕੀਨੇ ਰਿਰਾ ਰੇ ਰੇ ਯੀ ਰਾਯਾਰ
ਪੁਰਾਰਾ ਰੇਰੀ ਯਰਰਰ ਰਰਰ ਰ ਰਾਰਿਯਾ ਰੇਯ ਰਾਰ
ਰਿਰਾ ਰਰਰ ਰ ਰਰ ਰ ਰ ਰਿਰਰ ਰਿਰੀਰੀ ਰੇ ਰਾਰ
ਰ ਰੇ ਰਿਯਾਂ ਰੇ ਰਰ ਰੀ ਰਿਰੇਰ ਰਾਮ ਰਰਾ ਯ

The people who have resettled here continue to search for those they once knew—for old friends and family, for familiar faces from the villages they left behind. The refugees don't mix with those new to them. They cling to those lost connections, unable or unwilling to replace them with new ones. Even now, India and their ancestral villages live vividly in their thoughts.

Millions of people were devastated by this Partition. Even though many of them were allotted land after coming here, they still deeply miss their old days and their old people. It is not easy to forget the past — it is never simple. Many people remember the days before and feel joy in those memories. Some spend their whole lives surrounded by the memories of the past, unable to step out of them. Even now, when old friends meet, they feel very happy remembering those earlier times, recalling the old events and the life they once lived. Whenever the older villagers gather, their conversations inevitably drift back in time—to the days before Partition, whether they were rich or poor. Those shared memories have become their anchor and are the only things that make them happy.

When I arrived in Pakistan and stayed in our family home, the joy of the past came flooding back. I could feel *Fullanwar*—our old village—alive within me. When I told my good friend Kulwant Singh Virk about my visit, he was quite pleased, including that I had visited his own ancestral village which neighbored my own. The memories stirred something deep in my heart.

There is an old saying that captures it best:

"Yesterday's thorns still pierce, and even yesterday's flowers
can stir grief."

Page 3

Though many years have passed since the creation of Pakistan, its birth was soaked in blood. Countless Hindus and Sikhs were massacred, and many were converted to Islam. The hope that people might one day return to their ancestral homes never became reality. Hindus and Sikhs were resettled in India, gaining the properties for those left behind in Pakistan, but they could never truly go back. The Muslims who migrated from India arrived here with little—living in makeshift shelters of straw, without locks, without beams, without foundations.

Over time, those fragile huts turned into mud homes, and eventually, they became permanent dwellings within the villages. Schools were slowly established—primary, middle, and high schools—even if some were far away. Education became mandatory, and with it came new opportunities. Female teachers were appointed in rural areas, and gradually, a new map of the country began to emerge. This was the architecture of a free, reimagined nation.

India, after enduring centuries of foreign rule, finally tasted freedom—but at a devastating cost. The land was split in two. And the deepest wound of that split was religious division. Muhammad Ali Jinnah, the leader of the Muslims, demanded a separate homeland—Pakistan—where Muslims could live freely. He achieved that vision, but the price was unthinkable.

ਮੈਂ ਰੇਲ ਰਾਹੀ ਰੇਲ ਰਾਹੀ ਪਾਕਿਸਤਾਨ ਵਿੱਚ ਸਿੰਧ ਅਤੇ ਸਿੰਧ ਰਾਹੀ ਜਾ । ਇਹਨਾਂ
ਜਾ ਲਿਆ ਨੂੰ ਪਾਕਿਸਤਾਨ ਵਿੱਚੋਂ ਰਾਹ, ਇਹ ਗਿਆ ਤੇ ਰਾਹਾਂ ਦੇ ਰਾਹ ਦੇ ਰਾਹ
(ਇਹ ਰਾਹ ਦੀ) ਇਹ ਗਿਆ । ਮਾਤਾ ਸਿੰਘ ਸਿੰਘ ੨੧ ਬਹੁਤ/ਰਿਹਾ
ਪਾਕਿਸਤਾਨ ਵਿੱਚ ਰਿਹਾ ਗਿਆ ।
ਇਹ ਰਾਹ ਦੇ ਆਪ ਪਰਿਵਾਰ ਰਾਹਾਂ ਰਹਿਣ ਰੇਲ ਦੇ ਆਪ ਘਰ ਵਿੱਚ
ਆਪ ਰੇਲ੍ਹਾਂ ਰਾਹਿਆ ਕਰ ਰਾਹ ਦੇ ਰਹਿਣ ਰਾਹ ਆਪ ਸਿੰਧ ਸੁੱਖ
ਰਹੇ ਰੇਲ ਰਾਹ ਰੇਲ ਰਹਿਣ ਰੇਲ ਰਹੁ ਰੇਲ ਬਹੁਤ ਬਹੁਤ ਤੇ ਰਿਹਾ
ਆਪ ਰੇਲ੍ਹ ਤੇ ਰਾਹ ਦੇ ਰਾਹ ਸਿੰਘ ਤੇ ਬਹੁਤ ਰਾਹ ਰਾਹ ਦੇ ਰੇਲੀ ਪਾਰਟੀ ਰਹੇ
ਸਿੰਧ ਵਰਤ ਰਹੇ ਸਿੰਘ ਮੇਲੇ ਰਾਹ ਦੇ ਰੇਲ ਘਰ ਵਿੱਚੋਂ ਰਾਹ ਰਾਹ
ਰੇਲ ਰਾਹ ਰਹਿ ਰਾਹ । ੨੧ ਪਾਰਟੀ ਨੂੰ ਜਾ ਰਾਹ ਰਹਿ ਰੇਲੀ ਰਾਹ
ਰਾਹ ਰਹੁ ਰਾਹ । ਰਾਹ ਤੇ ਆ ਰਹੇ ਸਿੰਘ ਰਾਹਿਆ ਪਾਸ ਰਾਹ
ਰਾਹ ਮੈਂ ਰਹੀ ਜਾ ਰਹੇ ਰੇਲ ਰਾਹ ਪਾਸ ਆਪਾਂ ਸੁਖ ਰਹਿ ਦੇ
ਰੇਲੀ ਰਾਹਾਂ ਦੇ ਰਾਹੀ ਰੇਲ ਰਾਹ ਰਾਹ ਨੂੰ ਰੇਲੀ ਜਾ ਰਾਹ ਸਿੰਘ
ਆਪ ਰੇਲ ਰਾਹ ਰਾਹ ਰੇਲ ਰਾਹ ਰਾਹ ਸੁਖ ਰਹਿ ਆਪ ਰਾਹੁ ਦੇ ਰਾਹ
ਮੈਂ ਤੇ ਰਾਹੀ ਰਹੇ ਰੇਲ ਰਾਹ ਰਾਹ ਜਾ ਜਾਂਦੇ ਰਹੇ ।

ਤ੍ਰਿਲੋਚਨ ਸਿੰਘ
੨੧-੬-੨੦੨੪

Page 4

All the Hindus and Sikhs who had once lived peacefully in what became Pakistan were forced to leave. Millions were killed in the chaos. Our village, like so many other Sikh regions, became part of Pakistan. We fled with nothing to go to India—leaving behind our home, our land, and all that was familiar—just to save our lives.

We arrived in India as refugees, but life here was brutally hard. We faced hunger, poverty, and humiliation. There were times we had nothing to eat and had to beg for food. I will never forget one such moment in the village of Bular. My mother knocked on a stranger's door and begged for a piece of bread. The woman stared at my mother & sneered, "You refugees are just people we traded for Muslims." She handed a stale piece of bread with pickle to my mother, who gave it to me to eat. It was inedible. That memory has never left me.

For three years, until I completed my tenth standard, I walked past that very house every single day. And each time, the memory would strike me again—my mother, standing there with eyes full of quiet pain, handing me that bread. I can never forget the shame and sorrow of that day. That moment lives in me still, as sharp and real as it was then.

—Balbir Singh Momi
June 21, 2024

Pause for a Moment's Reflection

A Letter For My Grandparents

By Amita Kour

My grandfather, Balbir Singh Momi, was from Sheikhupura. My grandmother, Baldev Momi, was from Lahore. As teenagers during the Partition of 1947, when Punjab was suddenly divided between India and the newly formed Pakistan, they were each forced to leave everything familiar behind—their homes, their communities, the sense of stability they had once known. That kind of experience does not simply disappear with time. It changes you. It alters the way you see the world, the way you hold on to people, and the way you build a life afterwards. And yet, instead of letting that loss define them in a way that hardened or weakened them, it strengthened their commitment to family. It made them more determined to create a sense of safety, belonging, and continuity for the generations that followed.

My relationship with my grandfather was very special to me, and it is hard to imagine any stage of my life without him in it. He had the most endearing names for all of his grandchildren, and for me I was his *chiria*, his *chikoo*, and his *grandy*. Hearing those names in his voice made me feel known in a way that is difficult to explain. It was simple, and it was powerful.

We stayed in touch as I got older through phone calls and messaging back and forth. Sometimes we spoke for a long time, sometimes only briefly, but our connection never faded. We talked about his homeland, the history of Punjab, where our family had come from, and the deep love he had for his own family. In 2017, he visited me at my home, at my little cabin in the woods. He instantly fell in love with it. He told me it reminded him of his home in Punjab, peaceful, surrounded by nature, nestled at the foothills of the mountains. That moment stays with me, and always will.

My grandmother was the true matriarch of our family. She was strong, outspoken, deeply involved in all of our lives, and endlessly devoted to her family. She cooked every single day, made sure everyone was cared for, and held everything together in a way that was both powerful and constant. She brought structure, warmth, and a sense of order into our lives, and you always knew when she was there. Our family moved around her presence.

Together, my grandparents were the foundation beneath everything. Not in a quiet or passive way, but in a way that shaped the rhythm, values, and heartbeat of our family. They taught us how to care for one another, how to stay connected, and how to hold on to what matters most.

Happy 90th Birthday, Dad

Listening to your Partition stories and visiting Mom's birthplace stirred something deep inside me—emotions that have now found their way into this book. I wish I had recorded every one of our conversations. No one could tell those stories the way you did. You had a gift with words, both in writing and speaking, that touched everyone who listened.

It took me many years to complete this book. I began by painting the Partition—each brushstroke carrying the weight of memory and loss—and now, it has become this book. You couldn't wait to hold it in your hands. I still remember how moved you were when I told you the title, *Daughter of a Refugee*. You said I would carry on your legacy, and I still hear your words: *You are your great dad's great daughter.*

Your presence surrounds me every day, but I ache for the sound of your voice—the daily conversations, the comfort of sharing my progress with you. The book is finished now, Dad, but I can't tell you that in person. Your human journey has ended, yet you live on in my heart, in memories, and in the wisdom you planted within me. That seed has grown, and I know you would be proud.

As I hold this book, I imagine your face, your hands turning its pages, your eyes filled with emotion. That moment will always be missing, and it leaves me feeling incomplete. Only you would have understood this feeling, Dad.

I was planning to celebrate your 90th birthday with you. Instead, I celebrate your life, your teachings, and the love you gave us. I am forever grateful for the gifts you and Mom passed down to me.

Miss you deeply, Dad.

Love always,

Tanya

For Mom, Always

Dear Mom,

The whole family misses you more than words can tell. Your high energy and warmth filled our home, and no one could ever replicate your cooking. Your hugs held a comfort that we still ache for.

You were determined that your four daughters would have the best of everything. From you, we learned more than just how to care for our skin and hair; we learned that one doesn't have to be rich to be clean, dignified, and well-mannered. You dressed with elegance and taught us to value our own self-confidence and self-worth.

I cherish the time you spent with us in America, and I miss our daily conversations. I saved every one of your missed-call messages; they are a piece of you I can still hold. I remember you talking about the first 12 years of your life in Lahore—how much you loved the food, culture, and beauty of that city.

I am so grateful Dad was able to make your dream come true to see the city of your birth once more. Now, your clothes, and your mother's as well, will be in a museum exhibit—a statement to the life you lived before and after the turmoil of Independence.

Mom, we love and miss you every single day. You didn't get to see my Partition art or hold this finished book, but I know you would be so proud. The strength I needed to write these chapters, the confidence to tell these stories—it all came from you. Everything I create carries a piece of your spirit.

With all my love,

Tanya

My Mother (Housewife)
Baldev Kaur Momi
Passed Away Feb 27, 2016, Canada

My Father, Balbir Singh Momi
Passed Away Aug 21st, 2024, Canada

Novelist, short story writer, dramatist, translator, and children's author, Balbir Singh Momi, was born on November 20, 1935, in village Amar Garh, District Bathinda, to Bhagat Singh. Alongside teaching, he was also associated with the field of journalism. Having lived in Canada for a long time, Balbir Singh's notable works include: Jija Ji (Novel, 1966), Peela Gulab (Novel, 1975), Ik Phull Mera Vi (Novel, 1986), Masaley Wala Ghoda (Stories, 1959), Je Main Mar Jawa (Stories, 1966), Sheesey Da Samundar (Stories, 1968), Sar Da Bojha (Stories, 1973), Nokriyan Hi Nokriyan (Play, 1960),

Lodha Vila (Play, 1965), Shaheed Bhagat Singh (For Children, 1963), Lal Bahadur Shastri (For Children, 1963), Nawan Khuh Purani Laj (For Children, 1963), Phull Khare Han (Poetry Collection, 1972), Punjab De Lok Naach (Anthology, 1979), Vigyan, Sikhia Te Qaumi Unnati (Punjabi translation of Dr. Kothari's Science, Education and National Development, 1973), Toba Tek Singh (Punjabi translation of Saadat Hasan Manto's Urdu stories, 1975), Jay Kant Dian Kahaniyan (Punjabi translation of Tamil stories translated into Hindi, 1979), and Nangian Awazan (Punjabi translation of Manto's Urdu stories, 1980).

In recognition of his literary services, he received several national and international awards. On his personality and literary contributions, Dr. Karnail Singh Thind published a book titled *Balbir Singh Momi te Ohna Da Rachna Sansar* in 1999.

Bio continued:

Chairman Asian Canada Biographical Center, Ethnic Language Teacher, Research and Evaluation Officer, Subject Expert, Public Relations Officer, Editor, University Lecturer, Translator, Writer of 20 books in literature, published. Member (Judge) Custody Review Board, Govt. of Ontario, wrote Research papers for PH. D. on 1- "The Study of women character as depicted in Punjabi Folk Songs" 2- "Linguistic & Cultural Study of Tribal People of India, 'OD' a tribe, 3- "Development of Punjabi Literature in Pakistan and Canada."

My parents were not just refugees, they were heroes.

Acknowledgments

To my wonderful parents who suffered so much and still raised their four daughters to live with pride and ambition for a better life overseas. Your love of music, culture, food, and education gave us a wealth of experience that helped us build anew for our families what you had to forcefully leave behind. I cherish to this day the memories of our shared dinners over laughter, joy, and deep discussion that went long into the night.

Jaypreet Singh, I never thought that you and I would be working together on translating our family's generational trauma into the form of a book. I really enjoyed the process of making my dream come true as this project brought us closer together, healed unspoken wounds by connecting to our shared inheritance of sorrow and triumph, and had us crying while reading and transcribing the handwritten letter of my father's visit to his ancestral village years after being forced from his home.

I worked alone for two years to get the ideas off my chest and in the last 5 months your tireless commitment and long hours (including weekends and holidays) brought us to the completion deadline of November 20th, your *Nana-ji's* birthday. I don't have the words to thank you: you're a naturally gifted writer and editor and I wouldn't have trusted this manuscript to anyone else. I love you so much.

Amita Kour, you are brave, strong, and also an amazing writer who has been my dedicated helper since you were a tot. It was you who encouraged me when I started painting and creating so many new works by labeling the canvases, packing the car, and bringing them to the exhibitions. You weren't shy about telling people about my art, sharing how much you liked and took pride in my creations, and for helping me write my first bio and artist statement as a painter picking up her brush for the first time in 22 years.

You have been an unwavering support to your brother and mother as that has always been your nature. Even though you are the youngest, everyone you meet thinks you are the eldest from how you carry both yourself and the responsibilities of those around you. You are the anchor of the family: I have never met someone so mature who can light up and own a room with her beautiful smile and charming personality. Wherever we go, you effortlessly become the natural center of attention as a kind, caring, and empathic soul. I'm so proud to call you my daughter.

For their behind-the-scenes support:

To my sister Nicky, for taking me to my exhibition in Ottawa in April 2025. The roadtrip we shared as sisters was a first-time experience I will never forget. You made it so special and memorable as we traveled from Ontario to Ottawa to Montreal. You spoiled me!

Nasreen Aboobaker, you are my soul sister. We have so much in common with our stories from Partition that brought us close. You always believed in me and your heartfelt appreciation of my work, including takings hundreds of its first photos in your studio showed your commitment to growing my artistic success.

Margo Harding, even though we lost touch, you were an amazing angel to my children and opened our eyes and horizons to a previously hidden treasure of American culture and mannerisms. There is no generous soul in this world like you.

Hortense Beker, even though you moved far away, you stayed connected and still support me to this day. We have said that we're both each others' heroes and that will always mean the world to me.

Kathy McKay, we have come a long way together. You believed in me and thought I was an inspiration as a business-owner, artist, and mother. We got to watch our children grow up together and those are the shared memories we will always cherish.

Debbie Crouse, for connecting with and collecting my art. I know how much it means to you to have original canvases in your private collection. Thank you for believing in their stories. I am forever your grateful for you supporting my business during Covid. Everybody deserves a friend like you.

Aruna Peri & Family, thank you for four decades of friendship and sisterhood. You made sure our children always a had warm and inviting place to enjoy the holidays and that they had gifts under the tree. I can't thank you enough for being the one to inspire me to paint again. You are my number one collector and your early-on support changed my life.

With gratitude to my friends and community:

Aimee Bouchard, Amy Ellison, Amy Berryessa Robe, Anna Toledano, Anusree Roy, Arati Misro, Archana Behal, Arati Misro, Bhai Manmohan Singh and Bibi Amrit Kaur, Catherine Hay, Christina Zhao, Condoleezza and Clara Rice, Daljit Kaur, Darshan Ahluwalia & Family, Diane Carter, Dima Sutiagin, Dr. Anjli Dhar, Falak Rajput, Fouzia Farooqi, Gaye DeMarks, Gayatri Bajpai, Gayatri Vasan, Geet Gobind & Family, Gigi Boss, Gigi Kubursi & Family, Glenda Crespo, Gunveer Singh, Guneeta Bhalla, Hassan Zeraati, Havish Ravipati, Isha Singh & Family, Jagdish "Toni" Rekhi, Jane Packard, Jaswant Singh (Artist), Juliana LeDee, Juliana Poli, Kalpana Handu Guha, Kai Deering, Kalee Tock, Kalpana Guha, Kay Korbel-Metcalf, Kay Willson, Kim Black, Kumud Jain, Lakhvir Sidhu, Lisa Merriman, Liz Nyberg, Los Altos History Museum (and docents/volunteers), Malti Kuls & Family, Mary Swetka, Michael Granville, Mona Xu, Monette Toverada, Mr. & Mrs. Sukhmander Singh, Namrita Yuhanna,

Nan Geschke, Neeta Bajaj & Family, Noeen Malik, Porter Wong, Priyanka Paranjape, Prof. Prem Singh Mann, Puneet Sodhi & Family, Puri Family, Raj Budhwal, Rajeev Nanda, Rajesh & Rekha Behal, Ranjit Kaur (Dad's Sister), Rashmi Rustagi, Ritika Rose, Robert Mintz, Ruby Kaur, Sajitha Malik and Family, Satjiv Chahal, Sejal Prakash, Shalini Datta, Shannon Harding, Shyamala Chandler & Family, Sonu Singh, Sue Johanson, Sunita Sohrabi, and Vicki Holman.

Special Thanks:

To the countless clients at Spoil Me Spa Salon, Renee Burgard and the Sangha: Corinne Collins, Mary Desjardins, Ruth Leibig, Sandra Hietala. To Mattias Ikeda & Family, Ritu Marwah, Karen Napier, Tina Sivyer, and of course: all my sisters and their families. I love you all.

To anyone I overlooked: please know that your contributions, by way of inspiration, guidance, or assistance, are sincerely appreciated. Thank you for being a part of this journey.

Notes

www.ingramcontent.com/pod-product-compliance
Lightning Source LLC
Chambersburg PA
CBHW030412130626
46549CB00004B/1746